LIVING
BENEATH
THE
SURFACE

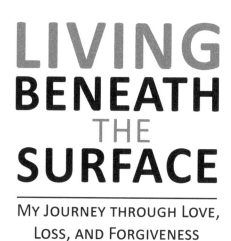

LIVING
BENEATH
THE
SURFACE

MY JOURNEY THROUGH LOVE,
LOSS, AND FORGIVENESS

KRISTA BENNETT-BRUNS

ELITE

Xulon Press Elite
2301 Lucien Way #415
Maitland, FL 32751
407.339.4217
www.xulonpress.com

E xulon
LITE

Printed in the United States of America.

ISBN-13: 9781545614761

"I arise in the morning torn between a desire to improve (or save) the world and a desire to enjoy (or savor) the world. This makes it hard to plan the day."
~ E.B. White

This book is dedicated to Bennett, Palmer, Mason, and Sutton Bruns.
I am so thankful and honored that God chose me to be your mom. I love you!

Foreword

LIFE IS FASCINATING. IT COMES WITH SO MUCH work, joy, growth, sweat, tears, and learning. If you are lucky, you are aware of the lessons amidst the emotion. If you are lucky, you can look back and see your growth. And if you are extremely lucky, you meet people along the way that teach you these lessons. I am lucky beyond words.

I met Dr. Krista Bennett-Bruns in a professional scenario. I am an endodontist, which is a dental specialty. My patients are referred from general dentists. Krista and I began working together several years ago. Our professional relationship turned into a close and treasured friendship rather quickly. I wish I could take partial credit for this but I can't. Krista has never met a stranger.

After working together on several cases, Krista and I realized we had a shared patient and practice philosophy of "people first." This means to me that what people are experiencing, feeling and are going through comes first before their teeth.

Krista and her husband, Robert, have the same approach. We are innately empathetic. It is who we are. Krista and Robert began inviting me and my husband to parties. These events included staff gatherings at their house, holiday gatherings, lunch at their office and to a group of their personal friends that gather once a month. Krista and Robert just included us again and again. These gatherings were always full of joy, and we always laughed harder at those events than almost any other time or place in our lives. They were continually hospitable, hilarious and just plain old fun.

As our friendship progressed and life happened, Krista and I continually went to one another with terrific celebrations and great losses. I lost my father tragically. Krista lost hers suddenly. I experienced multiple miscarriages and infertility. She had already been down that road as well. We helped each other through all of this. We discussed faith, parenting, business, friendship, marriage, and love. We have shared scripture, songs of faith, and our belief in God's grace. We are both extremely hard working and determined. We are both type A women who want to do the most we can, the best we can, when we can. We can be candid with one another and most importantly—honest.

Krista Bennett-Bruns has had a life like no other. The hurdles that have been placed in her way are like mountains. The strength that she has exhibited again and again is that of a superhero. Krista has taught me how to be a good friend. She has taught me how to live life to the fullest. She has taught me how to be adventurous, to be brave, how to dream, how to persevere, and to love without ceasing. I am lucky. Krista's story is a tremendous one. It is easy to focus on the challenges that she has encountered. The lessons are in how Krista handled them.

Dr. Gwen Corbett

Note from the Author

WHEN WRITING THIS BOOK, IT WAS EXTREMELY important to me that I not hold back on expressing my thoughts and emotions. There are a few places in this book where I use bad words and a few places in this book where I share what is on my heart and mind, and feelings and emotions that are not politically correct and may be offensive and seem very critical to some people. However, I find it necessary and pertinent to share everything—pure, raw, genuine emotions, feelings, and thoughts. I in no way hold back what is on my heart to say.

I had many goals when feeling led to write this book, and I felt led to share everything and pour out my heart and not hold anything back. I refused to re-word or re-phrase a sentence to cover up and mask my thoughts and feelings and emotions. I refused to sugarcoat anything in order for my book to be accepted. There is too much of that going on in the world today. It was imperative to me that my readers see that we are all human, and we all have this huge mixture of complex emotions and feelings, and we are all ALIKE in so many ways. But, most importantly, I wanted people to know that YOU ARE NOT ALONE! Although my circumstances are different than yours, I have experienced a plethora of events and situations in my life and can pretty much guarantee that each of you has experienced some, if not all, of the emotions and feelings that I share with you in this book. Just because I share the emotions and feelings of what was going on in my heart and mind at the time does not give me the right to act on these emotions and it does not make me wrong for thinking or feeling them! I am simply just being honest and not suppressing what I felt led to say.

If you want to know you are not alone in this world with the emotions and feelings and thoughts you experience, and if you want to see how we are all so interconnected and how beautiful life is/can be, even amidst our pain, tragedy, and suffering, and if you want to see how important and valuable each person's life is, including yours, and if you want to see how we all can make an impact on this world, then this book is for you!

I can pretty much guarantee that if you open your heart and your spirit to truly understand what I am writing, by the end of this book, you will feel better about your life. You will also be on the road to discovering the purpose for your life if you do not already know it, and you will truly believe that you are not alone in this world no matter what your mind is telling you.

We all affect each other in either a negative or positive way, and your life matters! I peel back every layer of my being and pour out my heart and express it in great details. This book was meant for someone. I am not sure if this book was meant for you or if it was meant for someone else, or if was meant for my children, or if it was only meant for me. However, whomever it was meant for, it shows full-circle the purpose of life and the purpose of our trials and triumphs, and puts life in a "big picture" format from my little perspective.

This book will change your life if you really sit and open your heart to receiving the message. Quoting one of my best friends, Dr. Gwen Corbett, "People need your book so they know where to place all of their life experiences, and they can realize and know everything is going to be okay." You will see that love always triumphs—always—and you will see what living a life beneath my surface (beneath my mask) looks like to me.

Thank you for choosing to read *Living Beneath the Surface*!

Chapter One

"So we look not at the things which are seen, but at the things which are unseen; for the things which are visible are temporal [just brief and fleeting], but the things which are invisible are everlasting and imperishable."

2 Corinthians 4:18 AMP

HAVE YOU EVER HAD THAT FEELING DOWN DEEP in your gut that life seems to be going too well and there is that uneasy feeling that something is about to go terribly wrong? I cannot recall the exact date, but I do remember it was in either January or February of 2015. It was a nice day outside, and my husband and children were not home. I was in my master bathroom facing the double doors that swing open from my bathroom to my bedroom. I opened the doors to my top cabinet to take a vitamin B12. As I opened the bottle of the vitamins, I looked outside. The curtains in my bedroom were open, and I looked out of the four windows and was in awe of how beautiful of a day it was. Although it was winter, it was a beautiful spring-like day in Baton Rouge. I even stared at the beautiful flowers outside and had an ahhhh moment—a moment in life where I just soaked up the pure enjoyment of being alive. I admired the beauty and the smell of a spring day in winter and just took a moment to enjoy existing and feeling completely at peace, and so full of joy for having such peace deep down in my soul. I smiled even though no one was around. I took a big, deep breath and stared out the window. I experienced this wonderful feeling of being grateful for life and so blessed, but this feeling lasted no more than two minutes.

Immediately after realizing my vitamin B12 tablet had completely dissolved under my tongue, that moment was shattered by an overwhelming feeling that life was going too well. I had an intense, over-whelming, negative gut feeling that something was about to happen. I became consumed with intense fear and sadness and immediately knew that another "life storm" was about to happen. After all, it was a feeling I knew all too well, that I had experienced many times in my life, and occurred before each of my life storms.

My definition of a life storm is an unpleasant event in my life—a death, an illness, an injury, or anything that throws a wrench in my life and puts me on a dif-ferent path. It is an event that requires me to learn a life lesson. My definition of a life lesson is something that I learn from my life storm that changes the way I think or changes the way I do something. It forces me

2

to self-reflect and look at the unseen world and truly learn a valuable life lesson that changes my soul. The older I have become, the more value I see in my life storms. For my life storm can not only help me, but the lesson I learn can also help my children, family, friends, or anyone else who is in my life or comes into my life even in passing.

I could not shake my feelings of fear and sadness, and the sinking feeling in my heart made me sick. I stopped and took a deep breath again, but this time it was more of a long sigh of frustration that my world was about to be shaken. Silently, I asked myself, "What am I supposed to do with this feeling?" I had obviously been given a warning about something, but I desperately wanted to know the purpose of the warning and what I needed to do. I started sobbing uncontrollably. Tears just poured out of my eyes. I felt such tremendous sadness in my heart and this intense sense of loss and kept on crying, yet I felt peace at the same time. Although tears dripped down my face onto my clothes, I made no noise.

I sobbed for about twenty minutes, and then I just stopped as if someone turned a switch and immediately made my tears stop flowing. Still in my bathroom doorway facing my bedroom windows, I looked out of the windows and again admired how beautiful it was. I had this unexplainable peace come over me that felt amazing. At that moment, I knew in my soul that whatever life storm was about to be opened was something spiritual and it was far beyond my control. I somehow knew that whatever was about to happen was necessary for lives to be changed spiritually for the better. I closed my eyes, and I respectfully demanded that God tell me what I was supposed to do.

I had this strong feeling that I was about to die an earthly death and that I needed to plan my funeral. I was sad to feel that I was about to be separated from my children and would not be there to see them grow up. I thought of how I would miss out on seeing them go to school dances and miss out on their weddings, if they chose to get married, and I would miss out on holding their children if they chose to have children. I thought about the intense sadness and grief that my children would feel by my death. I felt fear that my three boys and one daughter would be so young that they would not remember me when they got older.

Bennett was sixteen years old, and I knew that he would remember me. However, Palmer was almost eleven years old, Mason, my daughter, was nine years old, and Sutton was four years old, so I was so sad knowing that my younger three children would not remember me. I did not care if anyone else remembered me, but as a mother, the possibility that my own children would not remember me when they were adults saddened me. My heart burned with sadness knowing the pain my children would go through. I knew the grief they would go through and the void they would feel, since I experienced this void when my dad passed away on August 16, 2007. However, I was thirty-four years old when I lost my dad, and as an adult, it was extremely painful and difficult, so I could not even imagine the pain of losing a parent if I were a child.

My heart hurt knowing my children would experience losing me when they were at such a young age. I thought about how I needed to write my children letters telling them how much I loved them. I thought about all the places I wanted to travel to. I thought about all the things that were on my "bucket list" that I had not completed. I thought about my wonderful best friends and my sister and how much I would miss spending time with them and how much fun we always had together. You see, I LOVE life! I love living. Although there are tough times in this world, I enjoy life, and I try to live life to the fullest.

As all these thoughts were running through my head and heart, I knew there were some people in my life who would only be able to be put on a different spiritual journey if they lost me. I somehow knew my funeral was the key to this. I just knew it in my soul. My sadness and fear and pain quickly turned into joy and excitement that I was going to have the most fantastic and impactful funeral ever, and I was determined that I would "go out with a bang." I wanted lives to be changed for the better. I wanted my children and friends and family to celebrate life. I wanted them to see that life must be lived and enjoyed even though life has a lot of pain. I wanted them to see that obstacles in life must be overcome. I wanted to send a message of love, hope, faith, determination, and perseverance. I wanted people to leave my life celebration with love, joy, and happiness in their hearts and to leave spiritually fulfilled.

Although I was worried how I would die an earthly death and I was worried about the pain my children would experience, I was full of peace and joy and excitement. I felt privileged and grateful that I was given this insight and this feeling that I needed to plan my funeral. I wanted my funeral to be a life celebration. It was imperative that I get this right and do every single thing I felt led to do. After all, a re-do was impossible. I began to imagine the expressions on people's faces that I wanted to see when they left my life celebration. Knowing my children, family, and friends would leave my service full of joy and fulfilled spiritually filled me with joy and peace. I wanted to shine the light in my soul. I wanted the world to see light in the face of darkness.

Based on a few previous events in my life, I already had planned a good bit of my life celebration service. Maybe four times in my life, I had already planned my funeral, so I just needed to update a few things and change a few things and be extremely specific on the details. I already had a list of my requests on the notes section of my phone, as well as a copy of an email I sent to Monica Lyon Davis, one of my best friends since ninth grade, showing all of my funeral wishes from a few years ago. Immediately, I got my phone, and right there in my master bathroom, I started updating my notes section on my iPhone. Thank God for the notes section of an iPhone, is all I can say! I added songs, deleted songs, wrote specific things. I always wanted live music and not that piped-in old funeral home music. I did not want the tacky funeral home décor I remember from my grandparents' funerals and from my dad's funeral. I wanted beautiful and comfortable décor. I wanted kick a** music! I always wanted my service to be in a church and not the funeral home. I wanted food—good food. Since I love flowers, I wanted lots of flowers. I wanted people to feel alive, and I wanted the atmosphere to be so beautiful and comfortable and peaceful that they would focus on God and the unseen world.

I know it sounds contradictory that I wanted worldly things so that people could focus on the unseen world, but it was necessary to create the environment and atmosphere I felt led to create for my service. I spent about twenty minutes updating the details, and then I went about my day. I remember being exhausted emotionally and physically from sobbing so hard and from being given this information and this task, yet I was at peace and I felt so close to God.

Over the next few weeks, at random times during the day or night, I would add more and more details. I could be in the middle of a conversation with a person, and I would feel led to get my phone and add something to the notes. I emailed myself a copy and saved it on my desktop at work, and I even told Monica and another one of my best friends, Britta Rabalais Wilson (both of whom I am very fortunate to work with), that in the event of my death, my funeral plans were saved to my desktop at work. I felt as if I were secretly orchestrating this huge celebration that would affect people's hearts so intensely and in such an amazing way that when they left, they knew who God was. I knew in my heart that I had to focus on the unseen world and not focus on this broken and chaotic world.

Chapter Two

"Even though I walk through the [sunless] valley of the shadow of death, I fear no evil, for You are with me; Your rod [to protect] and Your staff [to guide], they comfort and console me."   Psalm 23:4 AMP

SUNDAY, MARCH 1, 2015, MY HUSBAND, ROBERT, and I left town to go to The Woodlands, Texas for my doctor's appointment. Monica or Britta would almost always go with me to my appointments, but this time I asked Robert to go. I made an appointment for him to see my doctor, due to some physical trauma that we both sustained in a party bus accident our friends and co-workers were all involved in. This happened in the middle of October 2012, going from Baton Rouge to the cruise ship terminal in New Orleans. The plan was for us to leave town on Sunday and return after our appointments on Monday, March 2nd.

Leaving our four children with a nanny was never an issue for us in the past because my children loved their nannies, and it was a vacation for them when we were gone. Our nanny of seven years, Darelle, loved my children so much and was so fun. She had a degree in elementary education and was a Godsend to my family. She cooked well, was organized, did crafts with them, took them the park and doctors, and helped with homework. She was their mom while I worked full-time, practicing dentistry and running a business with my husband. Darelle was the perfect fit, and she became part of our family and still is to this day. Darelle stopped working with us in 2013 when she married and moved out of town with her husband. However, she made sure to always find great replacements who all loved my children and took great care of them, and I consider them part of my family as well. Within the two years after Darelle moved, there were approximately three new nannies. Although my mom lived with us, watching a toddler overnight was too much on her at her age. My mom moved in with us about five years prior and has had her own attached living quarters to my house. She taught elementary school and was a guidance counselor in charge of many kids for almost fifty years. I had no problem leaving Sutton at home for a short time with my older three children in the house along with my mother. However, Sutton was a very active four-year-old, and it was hard for her to physically keep up with him, so I wanted a nanny at the house.

I arranged for one of the new nannies to stay with the children on the day and evening Robert and I left for Texas.

Something about leaving for this trip felt different. I had this nagging feeling that I needed to make different arrangements. A few weeks prior, my friend, Charlene, whose daughter had been in school together with Mason since Pre-K told me that if I ever needed her help with my children to please call her. Charlene said she loved my children, and she said she knew we had nannies, but if I ever needed her, she would love to help. When I was planning my children's schedule and arranging who I would ask to take care of my children, Charlene immediately came to mind. I had a strong sense to call her, but I ignored it. I knew she truly meant that she could help and I trusted her, but I did not call. I decided to take her up on her offer to help when I would be out of town longer than just two days.

I could not shake the feeling that leaving this time just felt different. It felt off. I started to cancel the trip or ask Monica or Britta to go instead of Robert, but once again, I ignored that gut feeling. Not wanting to leave had nothing to do with our new nanny not being capable or trustworthy—it just was a feeling I could not shake off.

As I headed out the door on Sunday, March 1, 2015 for Texas, I hugged and kissed Bennett, Palmer, and Mason. I also hugged my mom goodbye. Although I wanted to hug and kiss Sutton desperately, I knew he would cry and cry for his "Da" and me. So, the kids and nanny did what they always did and took Sutton into the game room or bedroom to distract him until

Robert and I left. After driving off, I felt so guilty for not hugging Sutton, but I just did not want to see him so upset and leave with him upset, and I wanted to protect him from being sad for a few minutes.

On the way to Texas, I was almost paranoid about getting in a wreck, and I was very nervous as I watched all the people texting and driving and not looking at the wheel. I watched the eighteen wheelers all swerve and drive way too fast. I was very comfortable with Robert's driving—it was all the distracted drivers on the road I was uncomfortable with. I attributed my fear of getting into a major wreck to post-traumatic stress from being in that party bus accident a few years prior, so I just prayed we would arrive safely in Texas. And so, I ignored the feeling that something was different.

On Monday, March 2, 2015, I went to see my doctor. I do not recall anything different about that morning. We went to our doctor's appointment. As with any doctor's (or dentist's) office, it was no surprise that the doctor was running behind. Some patients take longer than others. Some procedures do not go as quickly as planned, so it is easy for the doctor to run late. I understood that and sat patiently, knowing all the times I had made my patients wait. We finished with the doctor in The Woodlands, Texas and went to eat lunch. At lunch, I told Robert how much bigger and better everything was in Texas, and told him I wanted to move to The Woodlands. This was not the first time I told Robert that I wanted to move out of state. Although

I loved my children's school in Baton Rouge, the fact that our children had to go to a private school in Baton Rouge because of the many unorganized and underperforming public elementary, middle, and high schools frustrated me.

I could work less and get home before 7:00 p.m. at night if we moved to Texas and our children attended public school there. Also, Texas was so business-friendly that it would be financially better for us to move. In addition, Sutton, my four-year-old at the time, had special needs and the one phenomenal public school in Baton Rouge, Southdowns Elementary, was a Pre-K and Kindergarten-only school. Once Sutton started first grade, there were no good options for schools in Baton Rouge to meet his needs. Therefore, I felt in my heart that Texas was the place to be for numerous reasons, but especially since I had a special needs son, and the public schools in Texas were excellent and could meet his needs.

After lunch, I asked Robert to drive through a few neighborhoods in The Woodlands and even had him drive to check out the high school. Robert was very unhappy with me that I insisted we drive and look at houses and schools, but he reluctantly did so. He said on numerous occasions that he wanted to get back home. Robert was very much the homebody, and I was the one who liked being on the go. My close friends always joked with me that they never knew what time they would be home when they were with me. I liked to stop and sightsee or stop and go to places I had never been, so a four-hour trip might take me eight hours, depending on what there was to do along the way. Robert also wanted to get back home since we had to be at work early the next day, and be home in time to cook dinner for the children.

After spending a few hours driving around The Woodlands and me trying to show Robert how great this town was and how we should move and why, I finally agreed it was time to head back home. On the way home, I insisted that we stop at BUC-EE'S. My co-worker, Stephanie, told us how BUC-EE'S was the country's largest convenience store with clean restrooms and every snack you could imagine. Britta and I stopped at BUC-EE'S on our first trip to The Woodlands, and I insisted Robert see how huge this convenience store was. I did not like to shop, but Britta and I spent over an hour at the store the first time we went. There were bird houses and nice flip-flops, cookbooks, cast iron skillets, and chocolate-covered almonds. I wanted Robert to experience it. He was less than thrilled, but since we needed gasoline and wanted to use clean restrooms, he stopped.

The entire way home, Robert kept saying he just wanted to get home. The ride home for me felt way more comfortable, as far as me not feeling like we were going to get in a horrible accident, until about halfway home. I did not know what triggered that feeling, but I started to feel like I was not going to make it home alive.

I immediately thought of how I did not hug little Sutton goodbye and how sad that made me feel. The details from the day a few months prior—the day I was in my bathroom and felt like life was going too well—popped into my head. I immediately felt that it was "my time" to go. I did not say anything to Robert at all, for I knew God had a plan, and I just needed to accept it and be grateful for the heads up.

My fear returned. I did not have a fear of dying. I knew that life on earth was not the end of my spirit and soul, and I knew in my heart that I would go to Heaven. It was the fear of how I would die and what it would feel like and the fear of that split-second between life and the death of my body here, and of course, I did not want to have pain. I thought of my sweet and beautiful children again and how much it hurt my heart that they were about to be without a mother. However, I had peace in my heart and soul, knowing that God was with them and God was with me.

Shortly after this uneasy feeling that something was going to happen to me returned, I received a text from the sitter saying she forgot she had a mid-term lab test at LSU that night and had to leave at 6:00 p.m. She asked what I wanted to have her do with Sutton and the older three children. We were going to be much later getting back home than I told her. I started to call Monica, who did not live far from me, but I hated to bother her. Monica did so much for our family and for me and worked so hard, I hated to bother her even though I knew she would not mind. However, I calculated how long we would be until we got home, and it would literally be less than an hour that my four children would be with my mom.

I either called or texted my mom to let her know the sitter had to leave, and I asked that she and the kids watch Sutton. I told my mom we would be home shortly. Of course, she agreed. My sweet mom was always willing to lend a helping hand and always helped with homework and dishes and laundry, and the kids all enjoyed having her at the house.

When Robert realized how much later we would be, he asked me to call my mom or text her and see if she would cook something for dinner so we could all eat together when we arrived home. This way, the kids could eat on time as opposed to us getting home late and him cooking and the children being hungry. I told him that I would not ask my mom to cook and told him that I thought it was too much on my mom to ask her to cook and watch Sutton. Robert and I argued about me not being willing to call and ask my mom to cook. I was adamant that it was too much to ask her to keep up with. He argued that we were late because of me looking at houses and stopping at BUC-EE'S, and the children needed dinner on time. I was not sure how long we argued, but I reluctantly gave in to his request, and I called my mom and asked her to warm up something. She informed me that she could cook fish sticks and green beans—something easy.

Robert was on the Mississippi River bridge coming back into Baton Rouge, and our SUV made a loud noise and had an abrupt jolt and almost came to a complete stop for a few seconds—it felt and sounded like the engine fell out of our car. It was the most bizarre thing. Then, the car was fine. I remember thinking that we were about to be in a serious wreck. At this point we were less than forty minutes from home. I felt sick—like I needed to throw up. I became nervous. Shortly after that, we made it to our last exit and were less than fifteen minutes from home when I looked down and saw that I missed a few calls from Bennett. I turned my phone on silent for my doctor's appointment (nothing annoys me more than listening to people's phones in the waiting room), and I forgot to turn the ringer back on. No text and no voicemail. I then looked at Robert's phone and saw he missed two calls from Bennett as well. My heart sank. I called Bennett's phone, and there was no answer. I knew immediately something was not right. My mom was seventy-six at the time, so my immediate thought was something happened to her. I called Bennett's phone again—still no answer. I called my home phone—no answer. I then called either my mom's cell phone or home phone—no answer. I repeated the order of calling each phone— still no answer. I knew in my gut and deep in my soul that something was terribly wrong. The last number I called—either my mom's cell or my mom's home phone, my son Palmer, eleven years old at the time, answered.

I remember where I was when he answered. We had just passed our church, Healing Place Church, on Highland Road, which was on our way home, and were less than four miles from home when I heard Palmer say in a frantic voice, "Mom, come quick, Sutton got out of the house and into the front pond and isn't breathing. Bennett is doing CPR and 911 has been called. Hurry, Mom."

My heart stopped, I could not believe what I was hearing, so I asked Palmer, "What, what did you say?"

Palmer repeated himself. I remember Robert asking me what was wrong, and as my mind was trying to process what I should do, Robert was upset that I did not answer him. I ignored him, trying to figure out what to do. I immediately called our closest neighbors, Tim and Teresa. Tim was a former PT and Teresa a former nurse. I talked so fast and so frantically, Teresa had to tell me to slow down and calm down and repeat what I said. I repeated what Palmer told me, and she dropped the phone and yelled for Tim to "hurry quick" and run to my house.

Robert screamed, "Oh s***, Krista. I told you we needed to get home and not look at houses," and he then floored the gas pedal to get home quickly.

I then called Sheri, the neighbor next to Teresa. Sheri is a Certified Respiratory Nurse Anesthetist (CRNA). By this time, my heart was pounding, I was out of breath trying to stay calm and talk slowly and articulate my words, but I was still talking so rapidly

18

that I was shocked Sheri could understand me. Sheri said she would be there as fast as she could. I then called another neighbor one street behind us. I called Dr. Trent Massengale, our dermatologist, and his wife, Dr. Ann Zedlitz, a former ER physician turned dermatologist. I now know they thought we were at home and thought we were going to bring Sutton to their house, so they waited at the end of their driveway for us. However, once Dr. Trent and Dr. Ann saw the fire truck at our house, they quickly drove to my house. At this point, I was still trying to process the words that Palmer spoke, and the words just replayed over and over again in my head.

As Robert hurried home, I texted my Bible study leader, Dr. Cheri Leblanc, an internal medicine physician, and I texted my co-workers telling them what happened and asking them to pray. I remember being in the car, and as the car approached the fence that outlined the perimeter of our neighborhood, I looked to the open field to left and saw the flashing lights from the fire truck. How could this happen? I was always meticulous about safety. I was always worried about our pool, and of course, there was a gate around the pool, and Robert, the kids, and I always made sure the gate to the pool was closed and locked. We had locks on all the doors and always made sure the garage doors were closed. I was an OCD freak about making sure all the details were taken care of. My mind was having difficulty understanding how this could happen.

I then remembered we added an extra door when my mom moved in, and it had a lock but not a deadbolt. I never made time to hire someone to install a deadbolt on this door.

As the car drove through the gate to my neighborhood, time seemed to freeze. I felt like I was in a very slow-moving movie. All my senses were heightened. I was very aware of everything, and nothing in the outside world mattered to me. I did not think of work nor housework nor any of the thousands of things people, including me, think of on a daily basis. Lights seemed brighter, noises were muffled yet I could hear, and I felt time stand still. The closer Robert got to the house, the more I felt as if I were in a very bad dream. I kept telling myself to wake up and this was only a dream.

When Robert pulled into the driveway, I told him to run. I called Monica, and she later told me I said, "Monica, come quick, help, I need you." I remember calling her and crying out to her, and I remember throwing my phone on the floorboard of the car. It was dark outside, and the fire truck was pulled into the yard to the right of the pond and to left of the driveway. I can still visualize every detail. The headlights were bright, and I looked up and Sutton was on the ground, his blonde curls soaking wet, in his school uniform—a solid maroon long-sleeved polo shirt and tan pants and his tennis shoes on—all wet. There was a firefighter kneeling at his feet and leaning over him doing CPR.

Sutton's skin had color, and he looked as if he were just sleeping.

From what I was told, Bennett jumped in the pond and pulled Sutton out of the pond and started CPR immediately. I am so grateful for The Burke Cobb Act and grateful to Episcopal High School for teaching Bennett CPR as part of their physical education requirement. Bennett performed CPR, and as soon as Tim and Teresa arrived, they took over. I now know that Sutton did vomit and his color was good and he was warm when Tim and Teresa were on the scene before the firefighter arrived. Good color, being warm, and vomiting after drowning are all good signs. I now know that Sutton was in the water for what is believed to be two to three minutes maximum. Robert and I arrived shortly after the fire truck, shortly after the fireman started CPR. I have no recollection of how I got out of the car. I just remember Robert pulling up and me calling Monica, and then being focused on watching Sutton. Somehow, I ended up getting stuck in the mud on the side of my driveway and watching from the side as the fireman continued CPR. Mason, nine years old at the time, was lying face down on the concrete in her plaid school uniform jumper, just sobbing, I did not go over to her. I just focused on what was happening with Sutton.

Palmer's face was so red, and he was wailing and so distraught. I watched the fireman do CPR, and I noticed he was performing CPR incorrectly. I had been

CPR certified since high school, and I got BCLS certified every two years due to requirements of my profession. He was supposed to be kneeling to the side of Sutton. And, he was doing compression-only CPR. Apparently, there was no pediatric mask on the firetruck. Robert, Bennett, and I were telling the fireman to let Sheri take over and that she was a CRNA and we gave our permission for her to take over. The fireman would not let her.

I kept saying, "He is doing it wrong," and asking, "Why is someone not giving Sutton breaths?" By this time, another firefighter arrived on the scene. I was not sure if he was there all along or if he just arrived. I did not know why the Automated External Defibrillator (AED) was not used sooner. Everyone who is CPR certified knows that as soon as the AED arrives, it must be used immediately and is the standard of care. Using the AED immediately drastically improves the chances of survival.

I watched as the fireman barely dried Sutton's chest. I yelled out that his chest was not dry. I watched as the firemen put the AED pads on Sutton's wet chest. Everyone that is CPR certified knows that the chest must be completely dry for the pads to stick. Robert, Bennett, and everyone on the scene who was a medical professional, including myself, kept yelling calmly that Sutton's chest was not dry. I watched as the AED pads slipped up to Sutton's throat. Keep in mind that even my sixteen-year-old son, Bennett, who was CPR certified just for one time, knew the chest needed to be dried off and was begging for the firefighter to dry his chest. I watched as Sheri, the CRNA, knelt by Sutton and calmly and professionally tried to intervene, but her help was forbidden by the firefighters. I watched as the firefighter yelled very sternly and pointed and told the sheriff's deputy who arrived on the scene to "keep everyone back."

I watched as Dr. Ann Zedlitz, a former board-certified emergency room physician and now a board-certified dermatologist, ran barefooted, with mud covering her feet, towards Sutton to take over, and I watched the deputy forcefully grab her and pick her up while she was running to try to save my little boy. I heard the deputy in a very mean and ugly way say that he would arrest her and any of the rest of us who got any closer.

It is important to note that Dr. Ann Zedlitz probably weighs one hundred twenty pounds, was one of the nicest and most calm people I knew, and was always on the local television news as their "skin expert" and had recently appeared on the national show, "The Doctors." I watched the determination on Dr. Ann's face, trying to wrestle out of the stronghold that the deputy had her in. She was begging them, telling him she was a physician and was trained in Emergency Medicine. Simultaneously, Robert and I both yelled that she was who she said she was and we both verbally yelled loudly and clearly and demanded that the deputy and the firemen let Dr. Zedlitz, Dr. Trent Massengale, and our CRNA neighbor take over. Our verbal demands were dismissed, and Sutton continued to go without any breaths and still had the AED pads up by his throat. The AED could not read the information from the pads if the pads were not on the chest. It is really a shame when a sixteen-year-old is telling firemen that they are doing things wrong.

I could tell by the look in the firemen's eyes and the expressions on their faces that they were in over their heads. However, they still refused to let the CRNA and two physicians, two dentists (myself and Robert), a former nurse and a former PT help! I kept telling everyone that they were doing CPR wrong and kept repeating that Sutton's chest was not dry and begged to let the CRNA or Dr. Zedlitz and Dr. Massengale take over, but the sheriff's deputy kept threatening to arrest us. Robert kept begging and begging, trying to convince the deputy to let the physicians and CRNA take over. I heard Robert tell the deputy that Sheri worked in the operating room and put people to sleep for surgeries and how they were all qualified and that they all "are who they say they are." I did not want to hurt the deputy, but I wanted so badly to roll over him in my wheelchair (this will be discussed in later chapters) and knock him down and fight with him to distract him, so the physicians and CRNA could get to Sutton.

I started to go over and bite his arm and run into his legs with my wheelchair, but I was afraid of getting arrested for attacking a deputy and was afraid of being arrested and losing my business and not seeing my children. It is important to note that I did not want him harmed! I only wanted to distract him so that my medical professional neighbors could get to Sutton and take over and do CPR properly, but most importantly dry Sutton's chest and get the AED to deliver a shock. I weighed about one hundred twenty pounds and was in a wheelchair, so there was no way my little body could harm the deputy —the point was to get Sutton help. Fear stopped me. Fear of getting arrested—I had never done anything illegal except drive over the speed limit. I feared being on the news and my patients not knowing the full story as to why, and people not knowing that all I wanted to do was get the proper help to my toddler who was innocent and just needed a breath of air and his chest dried for the AED to deliver a shock.

I watched the deputy's eyes and lack of facial expressions. It was chilling to my soul and chilling to my spirit and chilling to my heart. His lack of expression and lack of concern was shocking and sad. I remember feeling such sadness for him. What happened to his heart and what happened to his common sense and compassion? Instant hatred came over me. For the first time in my life, at that moment, I hated! I hated the two firemen for not doing CPR correctly, I hated the firemen for not drying his chest properly and ignoring the authority of the higher levels of medical professionals, I hated the deputy for honoring the "band of brotherhood" request by the firemen and not using common sense and ignoring the verbal consent and demand that Robert and I gave to allow our highly trained neighbors to help. I hated the deputy's heart and hated his lack of emotion and hated that he could not see that this scene was different than the crazy scenes he was used to dealing with. I hated all three of them—the two firefighters and the deputy. I hated the deputy more—for at least the firemen were trying and not just standing around. The deputy could have called for a helicopter trauma team, or he could have opened his eyes and heart to see that the firemen were in over their heads and allowed the CRNA and two physicians to step in.

Most of all, I hated the owners of the party bus company I hired to safely get my friends and me from Baton Rouge to New Orleans to the cruise ship terminal for not maintaining the bus. It had old worn tires, which caused the bus to blow a tire at 70 mph, ultimately resulting in my head trauma—the only reason I was in Texas at the doctor. After all, if the owners of the bus would have followed all the state guidelines for a commercial passenger vehicle, there would have been no accident. At least if the driver had a seatbelt, which he did not, he would not have been thrown from his seat and knocked unconscious while our bus careened the length of three football fields, riding the guardrail of the Lake Ponchartrain Spillway (bridge).

I hated these people. For the first time in my life, pure hate and disgust for all of them spewed from deep within my soul and heart. All of these thoughts were running through my head as I watched Sutton lay on the ground, as I watched Mason face down on the concrete sobbing, as I watched Robert, Bennett and Palmer sobbing, as I watched Sheri, the CRNA, still kneeling at Sutton's head, as I watched our neighbor's children watch in horror what was happening, as I watched my wonderful neighbors praying, hugging, holding hands. It sounds so chaotic, but it was a calm, organized chaos, if that even makes sense. Amidst the chaos was love and prayers and support from my precious neighbors.

The ambulance finally arrived. I swear there seemed to be no urgency on their end. They parked way at the end of our long driveway. I saw Dr. Zedlitz and Dr. Massengale head towards the ambulance. I now know that Dr. Zedlitz was giving clear directions to the paramedics. Dr. Zedlitz told them to "grab the 3.0 tube stat and decompress the belly," but again they refused her direction and help. The firemen and EMS workers loaded Sutton on a stretcher and loaded him in the back of the ambulance. Robert insisted that the CRNA and/or Dr. Zedlitz ride in the ambulance and verbally told them they were riding. His verbal consent and demand was denied. The workers loaded Sutton in the back, and as Robert told them he was going to ride as his father, the ambulance workers firmly yelled, "We got this" and immediately shut the back doors, and took off, leaving our CRNA, two physicians and Robert behind. Dr. Zedlitz informed me she touched Sutton's foot as the EMS workers were loading him and he was still warm, had good color, and his skin felt good.

Dr. Massengale later told me that he watched one of the EMS workers attempt to put a tube in Sutton's nose to intubate him in the back of the ambulance, but could not get it and he did not see them attempt again, and then the ambulance drove off. Again, the CRNA intubates people all day long and has way more experience than a paramedic or EMT. The CRNA or Dr. Zedlitz should have been allowed to ride and should have been allowed to call the orders and work together with the paramedics as a team.

In my heart, it appeared that there was a struggle for power from the firefighters and paramedics and deputy—that is just my perception. I felt that the firefighters and EMS wanted to save the day and ignored the physicians and CRNA as a power struggle. I also feel that our local EMS team did not have as much training as another private ambulance company in the area. I now know that many physicians in town have complained about our local EMS and their lack of training, and that the city has ignored the physicians' input. Several medical professionals that have worked in the ER at different hospitals in town have told me that they always cringed when they were on call and the "red truck pulled up to the ER doors instead of the green truck."

Looking back, I can understand keeping everyone back and not believing if someone was a medical professional if a medical event happened in a large event like a college football game or a concert or if there were a large party with alcohol on the scene. I completely understand that, but this happened in a very small, very affluent, gated neighborhood where almost half of people living the neighborhood consisted of physicians or some type of medical professional. On a Monday evening when everyone was calm and professional and the scene was safe, the deputy should have been aware enough to know that the right thing to do was let the physicians help and not deny a four-year-old boy professional medical attention when both parents gave verbal consent to let trained professional neighbors take over.

The deputy refused to let my mom leave the house and told her she had to stay for questioning. When I realized my sweet mother was denied the ability to come be with her grandson and my older three children and me, my anger intensified.

I am not sure who I rode to the hospital with, but I was told that Monica drove me to the hospital. As soon as I arrived, I told the lady at the desk inside the ER my name and that I was Sutton's mom, and I was escorted to a room where Robert and a police officer were. Sutton was right next door to us in a trauma room, but we could not see him. Robert was sitting in a chair and sobbing and wiping his eyes, trying to replay the events and answer the questions of the police officer as to what happened. I came in when

Robert was telling the officer that the firefighters and deputy refused to let the CRNA and physicians in our neighborhood help. I was furious that the police officer was trying to get information for his report when our focus was on Sutton and praying and trying to process what was happening.

Bennett, Palmer, and Mason were sobbing, and Robert and I were sobbing, and we were all in such shock. Shortly afterwards, Dr. Cheri Leblanc arrived and her husband, Joe, along with a sweet lady who was the chaplain of Our Lady of the Lake Hospital (OLOL). The chaplain asked if she could pray with us, and of course, we gladly accepted her willingness to pray. Robert, my three older children, Dr. Cheri, Joe, the chaplain, and I all grabbed hands. I remember holding hands and remember that someone prayed, but I do not remember anything at all during that prayer other than being in a circle holding hands and praying. What I do remember is the split second we released hands, the door of the room we were in flew open, and the pediatric ER physician smiled and said, "We have a pulse," and "It is not much and we have a long way to go, but we have a pulse." Our hands had not even dropped down by our sides yet, and I knew God answered our prayers. At that moment, I felt in my heart that Sutton was going to be fine and he would survive. I felt in my soul everything was going to be okay. Although I was sad and in shock and angry at the people who were supposed to serve and protect, I had an unexplainable peace come over me.

I immediately remembered the story that my pastor, Mike Haman, preached on just a few weeks prior. The sermon was about a boy who lived up north and fell into a frozen pond and was trapped for almost twenty minutes, and how the boy survived and how the attending ER physician who had no spiritual beliefs told the boy's mom that the survival of the boy was a true miracle from God. The story of the miracle and the way the ER physician's life and his spiritual beliefs changed for the better ended up on the cover of a national magazine. Amidst all the pain and heartache of the night, this story that Pastor Mike preached on popped into my mind. I interpreted it as a sign that God was using Sutton and going to perform a miracle and save him so that lives would be changed for the better as a result of Sutton's healing from drowning. I went out of the ER to where my neighbors had filled the hallways and the waiting room. The hospital had graciously moved my neighbors, friends, and members of my church family to a huge room. I told them that we had prayed and as soon as we dropped hands, the ER physician flung the door open and Sutton finally had a pulse.

There were about thirty people there—my neighbors and their kids, Monica, Britta, and Gwen, members of my Bible study group, Robert's brother who worked at the hospital at the time, and the mom of one of my coworkers. Everyone was so calm and respectful and well-mannered and quiet. Sadness and fear and worry were written all over their faces as tears streamed down. There was so much love and support in that room. I remember crying and complaining that my foot hurt, so one of my friends unzipped my boot and took it off for me. I have no idea why at a time like this, when my beautiful son was in the process of being resuscitated, that I was complaining about my foot hurting. But, I am grateful for my friend who unzipped my boot and took it off. After my friends hugged me and prayed, I went back into the room that Robert and my older three children were in.

After I replayed that sermon in my head, the ER physician came back in the room and said we could see Sutton briefly. I went in the room next door and saw all the monitors and tubes Sutton was hooked up to. I saw his beautiful angelic face and porcelain skin. I saw a lady on top of the stretcher doing CPR. I smelled the chemicals in the room—a medicine smell in the room and another weird smell radiating from the room. My friends always picked on me that I had a nose like a dog and could smell things from a mile away and could smell things that most people could not smell, but I remember the smell in that room like it was yesterday. It was the smell of an operating room after waking up from surgery and smelling like anesthesia. The smell was so strong that I could taste it in the air. I had a horrible taste in my mouth. It made me want to vomit.

Everyone on the trauma team was calm, had compassion, and they were working so diligently. They were very kind to my family and me. They were visibly upset but had love and compassion in their eyes. I could feel that they genuinely cared about Sutton and were working so hard to save him.

I went to the right of the stretcher and got as close as I could. I held Sutton's hand while they worked on him, yet I still had a peace that he was going to make it and be fine. I prayed to God that He would heal Sutton and use this miracle He was about to perform to show Jesus to the world and prayed for lives to be eternally changed for the better. I cried, I was in shock, and I was angry at the emergency personnel who came to my house. I was mad at myself for going to look at houses. I was mad at Robert for demanding that I ask my mom to cook while she watched Sutton. However, I can honestly say I was never mad at God, and I had peace and hope at that moment, even as tears poured down my face.

We were quickly escorted back to the room next door to wait.

I do not know what happened between us leaving the room from seeing Sutton and the ER physician coming back in. I do remember Robert asking the ER physician if they got all of the water out of Sutton's lungs.

And I remember the ER physician saying, "What water?"

Then, I remember Robert telling the physician that Sutton got in our pond. The ER physician did not know anything about that. Robert asked, "The paramedics did not tell anyone that Sutton was drowning?"

I do not know the physician's response. All I know is that the ER physician told us he was the one who got the tube in and that EMS never got the tube in and we needed to come see Sutton. As I went in, the look of despair and hopelessness on the trauma team's faces told me that it was not good. However, I never lost hope and was just waiting on God to perform His miracle—I knew without a doubt that God was about to show up and show off.

Robert, Bennett, Palmer, Mason, Dr. Cheri, Monica, Britta, Gwen, and Pastor Mike, and the entire trauma team and I were all in the room with Sutton. I remember Pastor Mike walking in, and I watched his face when he saw Sutton. His mouth dropped open, he covered his mouth with his right hand, all while tears were pouring down his face. I reminded Pastor Mike of the sermon he preached about the boy falling into the ice and being under water for twenty minutes. I told about how God performed a medical miracle and the boy was completely normal and fine. I knew Sutton was going to be a miracle. I asked Pastor Mike to pray that Sutton would be fine and healed. I remember as Pastor Mike cried out to God, begging for a miracle. He prayed with such passion.

The ER physician started giving me the facts about how long they had been working on Sutton—I want to say it was hours that they worked on him. He told me of how Sutton's body was small and how they gave him as much medicine as they could. A nurse put her arms around me as the ER physician signaled it was time to stop CPR and cease all resuscitation efforts.

At one point, I was in the hallway, looking into the room Sutton was in, and a female pediatric physician stood to the left of me and informed me that they felt like they "were interfering" at that point—I interpreted this to mean interfering with God. I begged in a calm voice for them to please continue. I begged God to save Sutton. I said, "Please, God. Please, God," over and over.

The doctor called Sutton's time of death. I did not realize it, but I now know that when the doctor called the time of Sutton's death, another doctor had to come get Robert since he was having chest pains.

A nurse said she needed to ask me a question. Without asking what her question was and without giving her time to talk, I said, "Yes, I would like to donate Sutton's organs to be used to save other children." I really wanted Sutton's organs to be donated— it was important to me for Sutton's organs to be used to save others' lives or give them sight by using his corneas. Unfortunately, they could not use any of his organs. I now know that it is rare that organs can be used from drowning victims. I was so upset when I found out that his organs could not be used to help.

She gave me a sweet and respectful smile, and the trauma team smiled at me and the nurse said, "No, that was not the question I was going to ask."

She wanted to know if it was okay to cut some of his beautiful, blonde curls off for me to save, and if she could take his hand print and foot print, and if it was okay for her to clean him up. I, of course, agreed and thanked her. She assured me she would stay in the room with Sutton and not leave him alone. I begged to hold him, but the ER physician kindly refused my request and said I could not hold him and that it was against hospital policy since they needed x-rays etc. and I could not hold him. I wanted to scream out, "**** your policies," and "What kind of person and ****ing hospital administrators and doctors are you to not let me hold my sweet boy one last time?"

But God quickly reminded me that I had a cross on my necklace and reminded me that I just had my pastor pray out loud, so I decided that it was best to be the better person and be different and not cause a scene. But really, how horrible is this policy that a mother cannot hold her dead toddler? I did not even hug him or kiss him goodbye the previous day. I just needed to hold him and hug him one last time. Touching his arm and his foot and his beautiful face while he lay on a stretcher was not enough. I needed to hold him one last time. I wanted to feel his head on my shoulder. I wanted to wrap my arms around him. I watched as dirty brown water from the pond trickled slowly from his nostrils. I felt his body getting slightly firm, I felt his skin getting cooler, I smelled the medicine in his hair. Sutton looked like he was sleeping.

I was told it was time to leave the room. I did not want to leave Sutton. A man in scrubs, who had been working on Sutton, approached me. He said he wanted to introduce himself. He told me I knew his wife and told me his wife's name. His wife and I grew up going to church together. Her father was the pastor of the church I attended as a child and was the pastor that married Robert and me. Although I never met this nurse, the compassion in his voice was so calming to me. I knew it was not coincidental that the nurse who helped try to resuscitate Sutton was married to my former pastor's daughter. The nurse told me he would personally stay in the room and make sure Sutton was not alone, and he would make sure Sutton was taken care of. After hearing this, I felt more at peace about leaving the room, for I knew God was watching over me by placing this nurse in Sutton's room.

I do not recall who escorted me out of the room, but I went to the large room in the ER waiting room where all my wonderful family, friends, and neighbors were waiting. The words, "He did not make it," came out of my mouth. I watched the looks in everyone's eyes and the expressions on their faces as the words came out of my mouth. The shock and sadness and grief and pain from what I had just said made me feel like I was in a slow-moving film, like I was in a fog and that my inner-most being was completely separated from my body. I felt that I was in a horrible dream, yet I somehow knew that this was my reality. We all hugged, and tears poured out of everyone.

The sweet chaplain told us we would be more comfortable in the hospital chapel, so we moved there. More and more people I knew arrived in the chapel as we all sobbed and hugged and prayed. We were all calm and only whispers and sniffles from everyone sobbing could be heard. Pastor Mike and a few of the board members from Healing Place Church were there, along with members of my wonderful Bible study group. My best friends, Monica, Britta, and Gwen were still there, my sweet neighbors, my niece, Misty and her husband, as well as Robert's brother and many others. Time stood still. I had no sense of time.

After a little while in the chapel, I still had this strong desire to hold Sutton. Even though I knew that Sutton's soul and spirit were no longer in his earthly body, I had to hold him. I needed the closure of holding him and kissing him. Dr. Zedlitz and Dr. LeBlanc were allowed to take me back to the ER room where Sutton was. I was grateful that the nurses and a few of their team members held to their promise that they would not leave Sutton by himself until the coroner came. That meant a lot to me as a mother. I just had to hold Sutton. Just for a minute or two. The ER physician forbade it. I was so angry and sad—that damn hospital policy—my mind understood it from a legal perspective, but my heart hurt even more. I looked at Sutton and sobbed and cried out asking, "Why did they not let

Dr. Ann save you?" The smell of the medicines and the smell of death permeated the room. I touched Sutton's beautiful face—it was so cold, he was so pale, his body was completely stiff. How was this happening to me—a mother's worst nightmare came true?

Why God? Why did everything that could possibly go wrong, go wrong? Why couldn't I just hold Sutton for a few minutes? How could the hospital administration be so cruel as to not let a mother hold her dead toddler one last time? Why did the firefighter and the sheriff's deputy not let the highly qualified CRNA and physicians help? Why did I have to be involved in a bus accident, which would eventually lead me to Texas for medical treatment? Why was this happening, God? Haven't I been through enough, God? Why Sutton? Why not me, God? It was supposed to be me, God, it was supposed to be me!

Why did God give us false hope? Why, when we were praying in the room next Sutton for God to heal Sutton, as soon as we stopped praying and barely dropped hands, did the physician fling the door open and tell us Sutton had a pulse, only for him not to make it and die an earthly death?

I can honestly say that I was not mad at God. I questioned Him, but I was not mad at Him. I had been through too much in my life prior to this tragedy with Sutton and learned that life lesson through other situations. However, please know it is okay to be mad at

God!! Do not be embarrassed or feel self-pity if you are still angry at God! He loves you anyway!

It was time to go back to the chapel. My heart was even more ripped apart, knowing that the next time I saw Sutton would be at his service. I did not want to leave. Although only Sutton's lifeless body remained at the hospital, as his mother, I wanted to stay all night. I wanted to hold him and stay with him. I wanted to crawl up next to him on the stretcher. After all, I left without hugging and kissing him the day before—I did not even say goodbye! Somehow Dr. Zedlitz and Dr. LeBlanc convinced me to head back to the chapel. They were both so strong for me and knew exactly what to say and do to comfort me and keep me sane. I am forever grateful to them and to everyone who came out to pray and show their love and support.

Back in the chapel, all of us were in shock, sobbing, praying, and hugging. Pastor Mike prayed out loud. I do not remember his words, but I do know that I felt that deep peace that passes all understanding in that chapel. I felt God's love even amidst the pain and suffering and shock. I felt the love for Sutton and me and my family being poured out from the hearts of everyone in that chapel. I still look back and am in awe of the love I felt from each person there.

After a few hours of us all being in the chapel, the chaplain knew it was time to leave. I still remember very clearly leaving the hospital without Sutton. Coming out of the chapel, I wanted to throw up, I wanted to die, and I wanted God to take me and put me out of my misery. I wanted to hold Sutton. I wanted to stay with him. Coming down the hall out of the chapel headed towards the covered area on the side of the hospital, rolling down the hall, I looked up and saw Darelle, our nanny for seven years, and her husband, T.J., carrying their three-month-old baby, Paxton. The look on Darelle's face crushed me, for I knew she loved and cared for Sutton and my older three children just as if they were her own.

Darelle and T.J. and Paxton had just spent the entire weekend at our house with us that Friday through Sunday and left to go back to their town just a few hours before Robert and I left for Texas on Sunday. I beat myself up over and over again and kept asking myself, "Why didn't I ask them to stay and watch Sutton?" They would do anything for my children and would have stayed.

Why, God? Why does a child have to die when murderers and rapists and terrorists who have so much hate in their hearts get to live? Why not take them and rid the world of a person with hate in their heart? Why take a four-year-old who was innocent and was pure love? I had so many thoughts and emotions: I felt love for Sutton and for my children, friends, and family. I felt sadness, grief, heartache, and pain deep down in my heart and soul because Sutton was taken from me. I felt hate, anger, rage, and disgust towards the bus owners, firefighters, sheriff's deputy, and EMS workers on the scene. I felt disgust and hate for myself because I did not distract the officer and run interference so Dr. Ann would be able to get to Sutton. I felt anger and hate for the hospital, doctor, and staff because they did not allow me to hold Sutton. I feared I wouldn't be able to stop from killing myself to be with Sutton, though I knew my other children needed me. All of these emotions mixed together and all piled up at the same time. It was more than my heart and body could endure! I was empty, and a part of me was dead.

Chapter Three

"The Lord is near to the heartbroken and He saves those who are crushed in spirit (contrite in heart, truly sorry for their sin)."   Psalm 34:18 AMP

SOMEONE PULLED OUR CAR TO THE LARGE COV-ered area outside under one of the hospital entrances, and opened the door for us. I think Dr. Cheri and Dr. Ann and Monica, Britta, Darelle and T.J. were around, quietly organizing and coordinating how to help and take care of us. Their help was so valuable, and there is no way we could have functioned without them. I now know Britta and Monica went to our SUV and took out Sutton's diaper bag, sippy cups, and his car seat. They moved everything of Sutton's to another car to bring to our house, so we would not have to open the car and see the empty car seat, and so Bennett, Palmer, and Mason could all sit in the middle seat together.

Watching the car door open, knowing Sutton was not ever riding in the car with us ever again, was pure torture. I was in such a fog that I have no recollection of who opened the door for me. I stared at the space the car seat used to fill—a car seat that was supposed to have Sutton in it. Just two days prior, he was in the car seat, smiling and giggling, and now he was gone. Just like that—no warning, no notice—gone. And, I did not even get to say goodbye.

Monica and Britta offered to drive us home in our SUV, but Robert somehow managed to drive. I am not sure who picked me up and put me in the car, but I think it was Britta. They fastened my seatbelt for me and shut the door. I remember getting into the SUV and going in and out of consciousness, yet I was fully aware even amidst the fog and shock I was in that I was leaving the hospital without Sutton and without the opportunity to hold him. All I could concentrate on was that Sutton was gone, and I had a huge void in my heart. My heart hurt and ached and burned, and my throat was tight. I felt like my heart was broken in pieces and ripped from my body.

After getting in the car, leaving the hospital without Sutton, I have no recollection of the ride home, with the exception of the first few minutes pulling out of the hospital entrance onto the street. My entire body was numb. Everything was in slow motion. I felt like there was this fog or haze in front of me and I was watching and observing. I felt I was in a dream, yet I was completely aware I was alive, but I just existed. My heart wanted to burst. I felt so empty. I could not tell you the date or day—all I can remember was that time stopped. I could not think about anything. I did not even know my name.

The next thing I remember was pulling up the long driveway at my house—seeing the pond in our front yard and seeing the deep ruts in the grass next to the pond where the fire truck was, with all the sights and sounds and smells of the past five to six hours replaying in my head over and over again. I relived the entire evening in my head as if watching a real-life movie in a very fast forward state. The drive up to my house seemed like it took an hour, yet it was just twenty seconds. It is odd how the brain works—how I could relive, in great details, the events of five or six hours in just twenty seconds.

Entering the house, I was bombarded with reminders that Sutton was not with me. Every doorway, every turn, every room, there were memories and flashbacks flooding my mind. Going through the doorway into the house triggered memories of Sutton running toward me, smiling, and saying, "Ma," and giving me a hug. I turned the corner of the hallway that led to the kitchen and immediately saw his booster chair at the kitchen table. I looked to the left of the kitchen table and there are two large black and white photos hanging on the wall of Sutton as an infant. His big eyes stared at me as I looked at his pictures.

The next turn to the right was the game room—a room only for the kids—with a shelf-full of stuffed animals, a chalkboard on an easel, and the red, wooden kitchen set that Palmer, Mason and Sutton all played with. I had a flashback of Sutton in his chef's hat and apron, play cooking on that kitchen stove, just smiling and bringing me pretend food on plastic play kitchen dishes. There was his red chair, monogrammed with his name. And on the rug in front of the television was his "talker" he had just received less than six months ago. I was so relieved when I saw Sutton's *talker*. Sutton could say a few words but was non-verbal. His speech therapist from Neurotherapy Specialists set us up with Kym Heine, another speech therapist, who worked for a wonderful company, Prentke Romich, that had the best Augmentative and Alternative Communication (AAC) device on the market. Thank God, Sutton was the perfect candidate for the speech device. It gave him his voice, and he learned how to communicate on this device very quickly. The AAC device has a display and shows many words at a time

My concern was that it had fallen in the pond with him, and I desperately wanted to know what his last words were. Seeing his *talker* on the rug on the game room floor in front of the television was an answered prayer. I picked up Sutton's *talker* and took a deep breath. I pressed the button to "wake up" the *talker* and there were his last words, "Darelle Palmer Keira sunny." Keira was his teacher at Young Years Daycare prior to Sutton going to Southdowns Elementary.

As I read the words on his *talker*, I sobbed tears of sadness and loss and pain and emptiness, yet simultaneously, I sobbed tears of joy and relief when I saw the word "sunny." For it was dark outside, and none of us had ever heard Sutton use the word sunny. I had no idea that word was even unlocked on his *talker*. Knowing that Sutton's last word was "sunny" when it was nighttime when he fell in the pond, I knew in my soul that he did not suffer. I knew in my heart this was a clear message from God— that although Sutton appeared to die a tragic earthly death, I knew that Heaven opened up right there in my front yard, and I knew Sutton saw the "sunny" light from Heaven. I truly know and believe without any doubt in my heart and soul that even though Sutton's body fell into the pond and drowned, he did not suffer at all. He was protected and safe in the arms of God.

My mind transported back to the day in January when I stood in my bathroom and had a gut feeling that I was going to die, which led me to finalize my funeral details. Suddenly, I realized that the gut feeling I had experienced and the feelings I had that day were not because I was going to die. The funeral I had planned was not my funeral, it was Sutton's funeral. I also realized that had Britta's husband's oncology check-up at M.D. Anderson not been canceled at the last minute just a few days prior to Sutton's death, she would not have been in town to help me. In all of the years her husband had gone for his appointments, never once had his appointment been canceled by the doctor. There is no doubt in my mind that his appointment being canceled was not coincidental. It was divine intervention.

I am embarrassed to say that once I arrived home, I have no memory of helping my older children at all. I remember hugging them a lot, but that is it. However, I knew since Britta, Monica, Darelle, and T.J. were staying at our house for the week, they were cared for and loved and taken care of.

Although my body was numb and in a fog and tears flowed down my face, the thought of going to sleep seemed so wrong and selfish, yet my body desperately needed to sleep. I remember Britta telling me she was going to help me get ready for bed. I remember Britta filling my Jacuzzi tub and removing my clothes to help me get in the tub. All I could do was cry and come in and out of reality—asking myself if I was in a dream or if this was real life. I replayed everything in my head over and over and over again—every detail—flashing lights, sounds, smells, conversations. Every detail of the night flashed quickly over and over again. I relived that evening so many times. I remember she had to pick me up and put me in the tub. I heard her voice softly tell me to wet my hair so she could shampoo my hair. I heard her, but I could not do it. Her voice seemed so far away. For those who knew Britta, her voice was never soft—yet her voice was soft that night. I remember her kindly and gently saying, "Shhhh," in a comforting way as I cried out. I do not remember her words, but I remember feeling her unconditional love for me. Out of the tub, she brushed my teeth, dressed me, and put me in bed.

I now know that Britta noticed Bennett was not in the house and tried to find him. She and Monica found him outside, standing by the pond, just staring at it and sobbing. They both went out and talked to him. I was so caught up in my grief and shock that I could not even remember to check on Bennett, Palmer, and Mason. Britta, Monica, Darelle, and T.J. were all coordinating getting the children situated for bed. They made sure we all slept in the master bedroom together. Mason slept in between Robert and me, and Bennett and Palmer slept on the floor. Britta slept in Mason's room and cooked breakfast for us the morning after Sutton's death. I had no idea they did this, and I have no recollection of eating a few bites of eggs.

My friends took care of Bennett, Palmer, and Mason by being there for them, since I was not emotionally able to.

The parents and teachers and staff from Episcopal High School brought food and packed our freezer and refrigerator with meals. The school and many of my children's friends and their parents helped with homework and sent sympathy cards, gift cards, etc. Many parents whose children were friends with Bennett, Palmer and Mason took them places to get them out of the house for a little while and to help transition them back into reality.

I now know that Monica took Robert's cell phone and took my cell phone from us at the hospital, and I so appreciate that. Looking back, it was a blessing not to have to worry about keeping up with texts and phone calls. There were so many people helping behind the scenes. I am in awe of how much people reached out and helped. For the days and weeks after Sutton's earthly death, I did not realize how many people helped. I now know that before we left the hospital, Dr. Ann Zedlitz gave Britta and Monica a significant amount of cash and told them to buy whatever we needed. Dr. Zedlitz sent her housekeeper over to help clean, and my other neighbor, Sheri McKey, also sent a housekeeper to tidy up and clean our house. Dr. Trent Massengale sent his brother, who owns Massengale Landscaping, to fill in the ruts the fire truck made in the yard, so the kids would not step in the deep ruts and twist an ankle or hurt themselves. Other neighbors sent food, flowers and plants to help brighten our spirits as much as possible. The list goes on and on of how many people helped and all of the things everyone did to help.

It was not until the memorial service and the days and weeks and months afterwards that I could emerge from the fog and look back and be aware of how many people helped. One lesson I learned was that God did not intend for us to do life alone. Let me say it again— God did *not* intend for us to do life alone. Do not isolate yourself! You do not have to have a large quantity of friends—it is the *quality* of your friends that matters. I try to surround myself with positive friends who want to help me be the best possible version of myself, as Matthew Kelly says in his book, *The Seven Levels of Intimacy*. And for the first time, I truly can understand 1 Corinthians 12:12: "For as just as the body is one and yet has many parts, and all the parts, though many, form [only] one body, so it is with Christ." AMP. So many parts, each having a specific job, but all are equally important. Each person focusing on and being aware of their strengths and doing anything they could to help us—each person contributed something different, but they were all equally important to helping my family and me.

In the chapel at the hospital, I asked Pastor Mike Haman to do the service. I wanted it at the church I attended, Healing Place Church. Just earlier that year, Sutton started going to kids' church at the 5:00 p.m. service. The church assigned a worker to any child who might have some special needs, to sit there with them in kids' church. It only took two times before Sutton was thrilled about going. I am so grateful that the church had someone available. Of course, Sutton stole the show and quickly captured the hearts of his teachers at church. I also wanted Pastor Dino Rizzo, the pastor who started Healing Place Church and who positively altered my spiritual journey, to participate in the service too.

While planning Sutton's funeral, I was fully alert and conscious. The odd thing was that if I was not discussing the funeral and the details of the service, I immediately slipped back into the fog. I remember bits and pieces of the days after Sutton going to Heaven, but I only clearly remember planning the service. Although my world was shattered and I was heartbroken, I had an unexplainable peace very early on that I felt—that peace that passes all understanding. It was present during the planning of the service, so I knew again in my heart that God was carrying me through this. I knew in my heart that God was going to use Sutton's tragedy to change lives for the better eternally. I knew Sutton's life and death were to show the world Jesus, and I wanted his service to bring unity and healing and bring people together. As hard and as heart-wrenching as it was to admit, I knew very early on that Sutton's death was to fulfill the destiny of his four short years, and it was going to be a tremendously positive spiritual impact to anyone who attended.

Unfortunately, for the first time I could biblically relate to Mary, Jesus' mother, in how she must have felt about the death of her child. Do not misunderstand and misinterpret what I am saying. I am not saying this in a sacrilegious way. What I am saying is that after all of the years of studying the Bible and going to church, I never comprehended the pain and heart-break of Mary losing her son and God giving up His son until I lost my son.

I remember being in my den with the Pastor Mike and Pastor Ken, and I was fully alert. I was so coherent and so aware that I had a Heavenly assignment to do, I pushed the pain in my heart aside and stayed composed the entire time the pastors were at my house talking about the service. At one point, when I saw Pastor Mike typing on his phone, thinking he was not listening to me, I said something to him in a joking but serious way. Come to find out, he was actually taking detailed notes on what I was saying. I misjudged him because I did not know what he was really doing.

The evening of Tuesday, March 3rd, 2015, Dianne Evans, our family friend came over. She owned a catering company and had catered parties for me for fourteen years, and made the most amazing cold shrimp dip, by the way. She nicely insisted we all eat together as a family, and she cooked for us. I remember sitting at the kitchen table and Dianne serving us all and taking care of us, and telling me I needed to eat. That night was a blur, but one pivotal thing happened that temporarily brought me out of my fog. Dianne asked me which funeral home was taking care of the arrangements.

I told her that Robert let the hospital recommend a funeral home. Dianne said, "You know Dustin works at a funeral home and does that for a living, right?"

I said, "No, I did not know that."

Dustin was married to one of Dianne's daughters, and I had known him for years. He helped cook and cater for Dianne. Without hesitation, I immediately told Dianne I wanted Dustin to take care of Sutton and the arrangements. She called, and fortunately Dustin was able to get Sutton's body transported to the funeral home he worked at, Ourso Funeral Home in Gonzales, Louisiana. I felt such a huge weight off my shoulders, knowing Dustin, who was like family to us, would take care of my little boy. I must take the time right now to thank Dustin and Ourso Funeral Home. Dustin went above and beyond for us.

I remember Monica and Britta, Darelle and T.J. helping the kids, Robert and me. I remember one of my other best friends, Melanie Turnley, coming over the day after Sutton passed away. I hugged her. I know I sat at the kitchen table with her, but I have no recollection of what she said.

A few months after Sutton died, I had Melanie tell me everything I said and did. A few things she said, I could remember, but the majority of the things Melanie told me that I said and did, I have no recollection of. I know that when my children walked by, I would give them a hug and tell them I loved them. I remember Monica and Britta complimenting me on how I made sure to give Bennett, Palmer, and Mason hugs and affection. Sandy and Craig Merrill, my friends from church who retired seven years ago and moved to Arizona, flew in from Arizona. My sister, Tammy, came in from Colorado.

God laid it on my heart to hand out bookmarks to everyone who came to the service. My sister is an amazing graphic designer and did the layout and design of the two-sided bookmark that the funeral home laminated, and she designed the cover for this book. Kim Burleson, a family friend of Darelle wrote a poem about Sutton that I wanted on the bookmark (see poem at the end of the book). I also wanted a slide show with photos of Sutton, just as I wanted for the funeral I planned for myself. I am thankful that Darelle took tons of photos of my children, as did the other sitters or nannies we had, so she compiled a file with every picture of Sutton she could find. My older three kids and Darelle and TJ and Robert and I sat in the game room and looked at all the photos on the television screen to pick what photos we wanted to use in the service.

I remember Monica and Dustin asking me how many bookmarks I wanted for the service. I remember saying that I did not see more than three hundred people coming. The sweet Cooking for Christ team at church, with whom I had recently started volunteering a few times a year, to help the homeless ministry feed the homeless breakfast, wanted to provide the food for after the service. They asked me to give them a number of how many people I expected, and I told them no more than three hundred people just like I told Dustin.

The night before the funeral, Darelle and Tammy took Mason and Palmer shopping for clothes for the funeral. Dr. Gwen Corbett, went to Black House White Market and bought me a few shirts, to see which one I wanted to wear for the funeral. Britta's sister, Lindsey Delhommer, who owns a hair salon and does my hair, volunteered to come to my house the morning of the funeral and do my hair. Dr. Zedlitz hired a limo to drive my family and me to the church and back. A family from Episcopal hired a sheriff's deputy to come to my house and watch the house while we were at the funeral, because during the funeral for a family member, someone robbed their house. [Side note: I must comment that I just cannot believe someone would look in the paper for funerals and go rob someone's house. I had never heard of such a thing, but, sadly, it happens.]

The days leading up to Sutton's funeral were mostly a blur. I do not remember things like going to bed or bathing (I know I did bathe and sleep, but I just have no memory of that), and I do not remember eating other than the night Dianne cooked for us. As I previously mentioned, I was not in a fog when I was planning the service. This was nothing other than divine intervention. The brain works in mysterious ways. I cannot get the details out of my mind of the night Sutton drowned, and I remember and can still visualize all the details from March 2nd, but from the time we left the hospital that night, most things are a blur. Occasionally, I will get flashbacks and remember things about the hours and days after Sutton went to Heaven, but I do not remember much until the night before the service.

The evening prior to the service, my fog lifted some. People like Monica and Britta (and I still have no idea who else helped, but thank you for helping) coordinated an open house at my house with food. So many of my wonderful neighbors and friends came and generously brought ice chests full of water and soft drinks. The priest at Episcopal High School, who worked with my older three children and taught them in chapel, came. The elementary principal and counselor came to talk to Mason and Palmer. My sister, my mom, Darelle and T.J., Sandy and Craig, and Monica and Britta were all there. Both sets of my neighbors who also lost children, and who gave us such amazing support and advice, came. Jim and Marla Cobb came. They were friends who lost Burke, their teenaged son to heart failure a few years ago after he collapsed after football practice.

So much love filled the room. Everyone who came was just amazing to us. There were about sixty people in and out of the house that evening. I could feel the love in the room. Although my heart hurt and was aching to see Sutton, the peace I had was so comforting. I knew I was experiencing that peace that preachers talk about—that peace that passes all understanding, which can only come from our Creator.

I have no recollection of how Robert was doing, nor how he was holding up. I know he was at the house, but Robert and I were both so deep in a fog of grief that we could not even help each other. Robert and I started dating when I was sixteen years old, and married when I was twenty, and he was twenty-one. We went to college together and ultimately went into the same profession together, opened a business together and had been married for almost twenty-two years when Sutton died. However, we could not help each other. Those around us were the glue our family needed. Robert and I never once hugged each other and never comforted each other after learning of Sutton's death.

Although he never has verbally said it, I feel he harbors resentment and anger towards me over Sutton's death. If this is the case, I do not blame him. After all, I was the one who hired the bus that crashed into the guardrail of the spillway in New Orleans, which caused my neck injury, which was why I was at the doctor's appointment in Texas. I was the one who made the doctor's appointment. I was the one who insisted on driving around looking at houses and schools. I was the one who took too long shopping and looking around at the convenience store in Texas.

As soon as Sutton passed away, we were both made aware that the divorce rate among couples who lose a child is extremely high—apparently, seventy percent or more of couples divorce after the death of a child. I am afraid that Robert and I are about to prove that statistic to be true. Robert and I just grew so far apart spiritually and emotionally. All we ever knew was school, opening a dental practice from "scratch," running a business, raising children, and chasing after worldly success.

Robert is a great person and an excellent father. He is extremely intelligent and is a great dentist. He does the most amazing cosmetic dental work. Patients drive from out of state to see him for dental work. On paper,

I have everything I could ever ask for. The people who know me would tell you that I am crazy for walking away from a great person and what most would consider a great marriage. We love each other as people. We work extremely well together, but we never grew together spiritually and were not emotionally connected enough to make it through losing a child.

Everyone handles grief so differently. Grief counseling and counseling in general are imperative. Both the husband and the wife and children must go to grief counseling together and as a couple and as a family. It is a necessity in my opinion. Going to church as a family is important, in my opinion. Praying together as a family is something we never did unless it was a blessing before a meal. I feel that "the family who prays together, stays together," but we never prayed together as a family.

Both Robert and I were raised in a Christian home and grew up attending church and church camps. From the time I was a child and all the way through my adult life, I experienced several obstacles and went through many life storms. I will talk about all of these challenges later on in the book. The point is that at an early age, I learned spiritual life lessons from everything I went through, which prepared me spiritually along the way. Robert had very tough times in his life as well and grew up very differently than I did. My home life growing up was completely opposite of his. Robert and I dealt with things differently. I viewed the things I went through differently. It does not mean that I am better! It means that he and I saw things through different lenses.

Although Robert and I did a great job building a business together and raising children together, we both failed at communicating openly with each other. We communicated very well when it pertained to our business and our children, but we failed at opening up and sharing what was on our hearts. We both enjoyed going to dinner with friends together and hosting parties together. We were both physically attracted to each other; however, we both let the "little things" in our personal lives pile up and never made the time to talk about those little things. We also failed to meet each other's love language. Our love languages are opposite. I have learned so much by looking back. We both should have practiced Dr. Gary Chapman's *The 5 Love Languages*, and we both should have learned to communicate with each other on a personal level. After reading *The 5 Love Languages* and *The Seven Levels of Intimacy* by Matthew Kelly, I now know why my marriage fell apart after Sutton's death.

It takes two people to make a marriage work, and it takes two people to cause a marriage to fail. The little, petty things we should have addressed just kept adding up and were never addressed. These little things were not really an issue prior to Sutton's death; however, I believe grief causes a whirlwind of emotions that trigger things that were suppressed to surface.

We always made the time to talk about anything that pertained to our business and children, but we never made the time to talk about personal things and have heart-to-heart conversations. Open communication is imperative. In my opinion, being in church together and doing Bible studies together and separately are imperative. Emotional intimacy is imperative

I personally feel that the key to a marriage making it through the loss of a child is having a solid spiritual foundation, making open communication a top priority, and seeking the help of a professional counselor or pastor/priest, both as a family and individually. If you are reading this book and have experienced the loss of a child or have experienced another loss or tragedy and have not done any of the things that I shared that worked for me, it is never too late to start. So, please do not worry or fret if you have done none of these things. Also, please understand that what works for me may be different than what works for you. What works for me does not work for Robert and vice versa. If you are reading this book and have never experienced a loss, it is imperative that you equip yourselves spiritually and learn how to communicate openly with your spouse or significant other to prepare you for when there is a loss or tragedy. I am giving this advice based on my experience only. I have absolutely no background in counseling. I am only sharing my thoughts to hopefully help prevent someone else from making the same mistakes.

In my opinion, it is harder on the dads who have lost a child. Almost everyone caters to the mothers who lost a child. Very few people reach out to the men. Most men are taught at a young age to suppress their feelings of sadness and to be tough and to "be a man." However, I feel this can be detrimental for a man in his adult life when faced with a loss or tragedy. There are way more churches and organizations that reach out to mothers who have lost a child than to the dads. It is very likely that by the time this book is published, Robert and I will be in the process of a divorce. I respect Robert as a person, a father, and a dentist. I want him to be happy, and I want what is best for him, and vice versa. We will continue to work together, but for some reason we just cannot live together since Sutton's death.

I overslept the morning of Sutton's funeral, but Lindsey fixed my hair and helped me get ready on time. As we left for the funeral, I noticed a sheriff's deputy standing by his unit outside my house, and I had a flash back to the night of Sutton's death. I immediately became angry. I was about to go to church, and I had hate in my heart. The deputy watching our house the day of the funeral was not the same one who was on the scene, but I was still upset. I did not say anything, of course, but I recognized how angry I was. The deputy hired to watch our house while we were at the funeral was super nice and respectful. The expression on his face was genuine and sincere. It was evident that this deputy had a more sincere heart, and his eyes were not cold. I had a feeling that he would have been able to understand the situation and he could have been reasoned with and allowed the physicians on the scene to help Sutton. Why couldn't God have sent this nice deputy to our house Monday night?

The ride to the church seemed to take an hour, when in reality it was about twenty minutes. I could not believe that I was headed to church for my child's funeral. The world did not make sense. I remember getting frustrated that there was traffic. It seemed so wrong that life kept going on as normal while my family and I were suffering.

The limo pulled up to the church. Still in disbelief, I took a big, deep breath and got out. It was beautiful outside, from what I remember. Upon entering the church, I immediately looked up and saw Sutton's picture on every screen all around the church. I cried as soon as I saw Sutton's picture with his beautiful smile. I knew then that Sutton's service would be amazing and classy and knew it would be done well thanks to the church employees.

There were so many behind-the-scenes things going on that I was not aware of, and I not only was not aware of how many people were involved in coordinating Sutton' service, but I also was not aware of the countless hours of planning and preparing. I knew Pastors Dino and DeLynn Rizzo could come in from Birmingham, Alabama, and participate in Sutton's service as I prayerfully requested. I knew Pastor Dino and had been in contact with Pastor Mike, and I knew Pastor Ken and Mrs. Judy and Colleen who worked for the church, and the band and singers were all working behind the scenes. I knew Monica, Britta, Darelle, and Dr. Cheri and so many others were coordinating things, but I did not realize the magnitude of what was about to take place. Not until I saw Sutton's picture on all the screens in the church foyer before going into the arena, and the visitation began and I saw the large number of people who came, did I realize the magnitude of his service.

How could this be possible that I was attending my child's funeral? I saw the flowers on top of the tiny coffin. They were so beautiful. I could smell their fragrance as soon as I walked in. I took a deep breath and prayed for God to get me through this day. I had peace in my heart, but my heart was hurting at the same time. However, I knew that someone's life would be changed eternally. I went up to the coffin and cried. I turned around and saw my OBGYN, Dr. Sharon Lee, and I cried on her shoulder, telling her that we worked so hard to have Sutton. I then saw my uncle, and I hugged him. Next, Dr. Michael Castine reached out and knelt on one knee in front of me and hugged me.

"I don't know why, but what I do know is that everything is going to be okay," he said.

A few minutes later, Robert picked me up and put me in a chair the height of a bar stool, so that I was sitting eye-level with everyone as they walked up. I took a deep breath and closed my eyes for a second. When I opened my eyes, I saw the longest line of people I had ever seen at a funeral. I hugged each person. It was truly mind-blowing how many people came to give their condolences and to celebrate Sutton's life. I watched as grown men passed by the casket and sobbed when they saw Sutton. Everyone came together in our church to show us love and let us know that they supported us. As sad and tragic as Sutton's death was, there was beauty in the ashes.

I chose three songs –"We Believe", by the Newsboys, "Come As You Are", by Crowder, and the "Blessed Be Your Name" version by Matt Redman, to be played during the visitation while photos of Sutton cycled on the large screen high up on the wall in the center of the stage. If I would have known how many people were going to come, I would have chosen more songs to play during the visitation, because the line of people went from where I was sitting in the church arena in front of the stage, all the way out the arena doors, wrapped all the way around the huge foyer of the church, and out of the building.

One of Palmer's classmates learned all the words to the three songs in just two hours of listening to them over and over. I have lost count of how many people came, but it was at least nine hundred who stayed for the service and an additional three hundred who came but could not stay, so a total of around twelve hundred people came to the church. I felt so much love in that room. It is hard to explain how I could be so heartbroken and sad, yet I felt love not only from God, but from each person who came and hugged me. I felt so close to Sutton—even though I could not see him, I knew the impact he made on people, most of whom did not even know him.

The service was incredible. The singers and the rest of the band did a phenomenal job singing the four songs I chose—"I Can Only Imagine", "10,000 Reasons", "Amazing Grace (My Chains are Gone)", and "Oceans (Where Feet May Fail)". The songs all sounded exactly as if they would have if the original singers and musicians were the ones on stage.

I remember some of what was said, and sometimes I lost awareness and felt the deep sorrow in my heart. Pastors Mike and Dino did a phenomenal job of capturing the attention of every single person who stayed for the service and brought unity in a room of a lot of diversity. We cried together, we laughed together, we were sad and upset together. So many people from diverse backgrounds under one roof put their differences aside and came together to show their love and support for my family and me, and some heard the story of Jesus for the first time. The church generously made CDs of the sermon and video recorded it for me. One of these days, I am going to sit down and watch the service so I can listen now being fully aware.

Everyone who walked out of Sutton's service, including me, left the church feeling uplifted. Yes, we were all sad, but not one person walked out of that service who was not uplifted. Pastors Mike and Dino and the Healing Place Church singers and band were like a breath of fresh air for everyone's weary souls and spirits. It was like a cold glass of southern iced tea on a hot and humid July day in South Louisiana.

In lieu of flowers, I chose several organizations to receive donations in Sutton's memory—Southdowns Elementary, The EMERGE Center for communication disorders, and the Swim Strong program through Woman's Hospital Foundation. Sutton was supposed to start swimming lessons with Swim Strong—a program that Bennett worked with one summer that taught children with developmental delays and physical challenges to swim. I called in the summer of 2014 to put Sutton in the program, but they started at age five. They were going to take him in the summer of 2015 as a courtesy to me. Now, because of Sutton's drowning and because of the donations made, Swim Strong expanded their program to have a Swim Strong, Jr. program, to include children under the age of five. Maybe Sutton's drowning and the expansion of the Swim Strong program will prevent several other children from drowning in the future because of the expansion and awareness of the program.

Knowing all of this does not take the pain away. It does force me to see a bigger picture. And it forces me to ask myself what kind of impact my life will make. "Do I want to change the world? Or do I want the world to change me?" I do not know which preacher I heard these words from, but I thank him or her for these words. Sutton's life and his death changed so many people and altered their life course. The majority of people attending his service were changed for the better. And it only takes one person to help change the world.

As crazy as this sounds, I left Sutton's service feeling so close to God and to Sutton. Although my heart was in so much pain and I missed Sutton so much, I felt honored to be part of something so divine, and so honored that God blessed me with being Sutton's mother on earth for his four short years. Although I was in inner turmoil and at peace simultaneously, one question remained unanswered. I desperately needed an answer from God. The question was about the night in the emergency room at the hospital when the doctors and nurses were trying to save Sutton, and Robert and the kids and I were all standing in a circle holding hands with Dr. Cheri and Joe and the chaplain from the hospital praying to God for Him to save Sutton. Like I mentioned earlier, as soon as we stopped praying and were releasing each other's hands, the doors to the room flew open and the ER physician said, "We have a pulse....it is not a strong pulse, but it is a pulse." I needed to know why God gave me this false sense of hope. I questioned why God would do this. I needed to know the answer.

I reached out to Dr. Cheri, the leader of the "Connect Group" Bible study I was in. I knew she would be able to give me insight and wisdom to find that closure I needed. After a few days of her praying about it, she had the answer I was searching for. She told me she had questioned God too about why He gave us false hope. Her answer was so clear, and I understood it completely once she told me. Dr. Cheri told me that God did not give me false hope. She told me, "That was God's way of letting us know that He heard our prayers, but the answer was no." I did not like that His answer was "no." However, I understood that God indeed was letting me know He was there, just like He always is, but I needed to trust Him that there was a bigger picture.

Chapter Four

"Let all bitterness and wrath and anger and clamor [perpetual animosity, resentment, strife, fault-finding] and slander be put away from you, along with every kind of malice [all spitefulness, verbal abuse, malevolence]. Be kind and helpful to one another, tender-hearted [compassionate, understanding], forgiving one another [readily and freely], just as God in Christ also forgave you."

Ephesians 4:31-32 AMP

ALTHOUGH I HAD THAT PEACE THAT SURPASSES all understanding in my heart that Sutton was in Heaven and that he fulfilled his purpose on this earth in just four short years, I struggled with bitterness, anger, and resentment toward so many people. I was angry and resentful to the owners of the bus company for their negligence, in my opinion, and I despised them. I was angry with myself for ignoring my gut instinct. I was angry with myself for not hiring a private swim instructor to teach Sutton how to swim. I was such a huge proponent of children learning to swim at an early age! Bennett, Palmer and Mason all were in swimming lessons when they were three years old. By the time they were each five, they were swimming year-round competitive swimming with Crawfish Aquatics in Baton Rouge. We stopped swimming competitively when Sutton started walking, and Bennett only swam for the middle and high school swim team at his school. I did not want Sutton to be around the pool at crowded swim meets until he learned how to swim. How could this happen to me when I was a huge advocate of swimming lessons?

I was also angry and resentful toward my own sweet mother, even though I knew her intentions for my children, me, and everyone else were always good and pure. However, how could I be mad at her when she turned her back for just a few seconds to stir the green beans only to turn around and see that Sutton was not behind her. Every parent has done this—turned around to put something up or to stir something on the stove. This could have easily happened while Robert or I were at home. I was angry and resentful toward Robert for asking me to have my mom cook. However, my anger toward myself, my mom, and Robert paled in comparison to the anger, hate, and resentment I felt toward the firefighters, sheriff's deputy and EMS. Although the doctors and nurses who worked on Sutton at the hospital were so wonderful and worked so hard trying to save his life, I was furious with the doctor and administration at the hospital for denying me the right to hold my deceased toddler. I loathed them for almost a full year after Sutton's death.

Each time I saw a firetruck, sheriff's deputy, emergency vehicle, or heard the sirens, my body would tense up, and I would have flashbacks rush through my mind all over again. I would often burst out into tears and did not realize until over a year later that I would hold my breath until the vehicle passed or until I could no longer see the emergency worker or vehicle. I could go from laughing and in a good mood to full internal rage within a spilt second.

I knew that I could not truly be at peace until I forgave those I was angry with, but I had no idea how to push through my anger and resentment. I would just internalize my feelings and voice my anger and frustration to my close friends, yet smile to the outside world. Forgiving someone for hurting your feelings or stepping on your toe or accidentally breaking a glass is easy. Forgiving someone who comes to me and apologizes and is sincere and learns from the situation is easy. But how in the hell was I supposed to forgive so many people who cost my sweet, innocent four-year-old his life? How was I supposed to forgive the people I had no contact with, while my heart hurt and my soul longed to see Sutton? How was I supposed to get rid of this anger and resentment?

The crazy thing was, I did not show this to the outside world—I just pushed it aside and went about life.

I tried to ignore my anger, but there was only so much that could be pushed aside and there was only so much pretending that I could do. I noticed that I was very short-tempered and would get agitated very easily. I had so much love and compassion in my heart; however, I knew my heart could not fully heal until I ridded it of the anger and hate I had toward those involved in Sutton's drowning.

I knew, biblically, that I needed to learn how to forgive before it destroyed my heart and before it destroyed my spirit. To try to heal my heart, I read a lot. I think the first year after Sutton's death, I read almost forty self-help books. Many of the books I read were written by Joyce Meyer. I reflected back to the Joyce Meyer conference I attended approximately six months prior to Sutton's death.

****

In February of 2014, I began watching Joyce Meyer on late night television while recovering from neck surgery due to the trauma I sustained in the bus accident. Unless it was football, I rarely watched television. However, my surgeon in Texas told me it was imperative I follow his orders and rest. When I could not sleep at night, I began channel-surfing and stumbled upon Joyce Meyer's television show. There was an advertisement on her show about the annual three-day women's conference in St. Louis in September. I immediately felt led to go. I called a few weeks later when I went back to work and ordered tickets for Britta, Monica, and me to attend. The three of us flew to St. Louis and attended the conference. We all grew spiritually. It was an amazing conference. Our friendship was already strong, but the bond between Britta, Monica, and me became even stronger.

At the conclusion of the conference, Joyce Meyer warned everyone that we would all get home and many of us would face major life challenges. She encouraged all the attendees to continue praying, reading our Bibles, and growing spiritually. She said many of us would face trials when we got home and we would need to use what we learned at the conference. I left the conference prepared spiritually. Little did I know that just six months later, I would be burying Sutton. Attending the Joyce Meyer Women's Conference helped me grow in my relationship with God. Many of the books I read during the weeks and months after Sutton went to Heaven were books I purchased at the conference. Although I have never met Joyce Meyer, I am eternally grateful for her and her ministry.

In addition to reading the self-help books, I also listened to positive, uplifting music. Monica stumbled upon a podcast from a pastor and his wife who lost a child, and she had me listen to the sermon series by Pastor Levi Lusko, called *Through the Eyes of a Lion*. At the end of this book, I have a list of books that I read after Sutton died that helped me, in addition to songs I listened to and pastors I listened to on podcasts.

I had to work hard at learning how to forgive. I heard someone preach—I am fairly certain that it was Pastor Mike—that you know you have fully forgiven when the *sting* is not there anymore when a name or subject comes up. I could not get rid of my *sting.*

I would pray, but would get aggravated with myself because my mind would wander, or I would pray in bed and fall asleep just a few minutes after I started. My prayers were not eloquent and fancy like my pastor's prayers, so I felt inadequate praying. However, I learned from Britta to just talk to God like I talked to her, and learned my words did not have to be fancy— my words just needed to be genuine and heart-felt and honest. I started reading a short devotional each morning when I got to work and would listen to positive, uplifting music.

I did all of these things faithfully for almost a year after Sutton's death without change in my heart. I was so frustrated that I could not forgive. Almost every evening, after my children were in bed, I would get in the bathtub and spend over an hour in the tub, soaking and listening to music. I would cry out to God—crying because my heart missed Sutton, but also crying out to God to help me forgive.

I like peace and harmony, and I like when everyone is happy. I felt ashamed of myself for not being able to forgive. I kept on with what I was doing, but after some advice from friends, I began to pray for those who had been involved. I did not know their names, but I prayed for each emergency staff member and physician who worked the night we lost Sutton. I must say I was not happy in my heart that I was praying for them, but friends kept encouraging me to pray anyway, so I did.

I would tell God, "Be with the firefighters, the deputy, and the hospital staff who would not let me hold Sutton." I could not bring myself to pray about anything specific. I eventually got to the point where I prayed more specifically—asking God to bring peace to them, and that whatever happened to make the deputy's heart so cold and hardened, that God would soften his heart.

A month or two before the first anniversary of Sutton's death, I started getting anxiety about the one-year mark. I wanted to do something special, but I did not know what. I texted a few of the moms who lost children whom I had become close to, and asked them what they did for the one-year anniversary. They all gave me details and encouraged me to do what I wanted. The one-year anniversary was really about what was on my heart to do. I stressed over what to do. I had no clue, since there is no rule book written for parents who have lost children.

One day on my way to work (I looked back at my text messages, and the date was February 25, 2016)—there was a beautiful sunrise as I was leaving the neighborhood. Robert and I were riding to work together, but we did not talk much. Just before leaving the neighborhood, God laid it on my heart to have a memorial service at the house. I did not say anything to anyone and just kind of started planning what was on my heart. My plan, as I looked up at the sky and the beautiful sunrise, was to have my coworkers and the members of my Bible study group over to the house to join Robert, our three children, my mom and me for a small gathering. Someone would give a brief uplifting sermon in memory of Sutton and then we would have some appetizers and finger food afterward—thirty-five people at the most. I must tell you that my plan was something small. But, on the ride to work, my plan got a little larger.

Shortly after arriving at work and seeing a patient or two, I sent the following unedited text message to Pastors Mike and Rachel Haman:

"Good Morning Rachel and Mike! As you know the one year anniversary of Sutton going to Heaven is on Wednesday, March 2. It literally takes my breath away to know it has been a year—part of my heart feels like it was yesterday and the other part looks back in disbelief that it has been a year...and I ask myself "how did we get here?" I have had a lot of anxiety about the upcoming anniversary date—anxiety from the fact that at the 1 year date, it is a significant milestone in our lives and the other part of my anxiety is that I feel led to do something impactful for this date and was at a loss as to what to do. A very small part of my heart wants to stay in bed and have a "pity party" and cry all day, but I know deep in my heart this is not what God wants me to do and that would take away from the miracle of Sutton's little life. I have been thinking of what to do, and this morning, God laid it on my heart to invite all of our neighbors and close friends and our HPC Connect group to come to our house the early evening of Wednesday, March 2. I know it is a church night, but is there any way you could do a short sermon and some music and we can have a mini church service at our house, and afterwards release 2 doves at the pond site? I would have food after. I do not want bother either of you at all—you have done so much for us. So please let me know your thoughts. I think there would be about 50 people there??? Maybe a few more. Just let me know your thoughts please. I do not get offended so please be honest."

Little did I know that God had something much, much larger and much more elegant and much more amazing and much more spiritually impactful planned.

I laugh now as I am writing this—at how I could not see, at the time I was planning this, the big picture of what God had in store for this memorial service. However, as the days leading up to the memorial service got closer, my spiritual eyes were opened wider and my heart could see what God had in mind in memory of my sweet Sutton.

What started out as thirty-five people and just some finger food and a few minutes of a positive message in my plan turned into the most amazing, beautiful, peaceful memorial service imaginable, with over two hundred people invited. I started making a list on the notes section of my phone—again, thank God for the notes feature—of everyone I wanted to invite. The list got longer and longer. Two hundred or more people later, I was in shock when I finally completed the list. What in the world was I going to do with two hundred people? I might as well have invited the twelve hundred or more people who came to his service, but I had nowhere to put them, so I had to stop inviting people.

With only a few days of notice, I had to call my friend, Doug Olinde, who rents out tents, chairs and tables for parties. My usual caterer, Dianne, had just lost her husband to cancer the same year Sutton died, so there was no way I was going to ask her to cook. I remembered going to Bennett's swim team dinner at another parent's house, and the dinner they catered was fantastic. So, I got the caterer's contact information and ordered enough food to feed everyone. They also provided the plates and utensils and sent two servers. I also needed two doves to release. In my rainbow and unicorn mind—as my friends will say—I envisioned releasing two, captive white doves into the world to be free together. Little did I know that when people hired someone to do a dove release, they were trained to fly back to their owner's home. That was not what I envisioned.

After I realized that the dove release was not what I wanted, Monica hopped online and found a company that sold butterflies. She called just as they were about to close and explained my situation and what I wanted to do. She wrote down all of the details for me and told me how the process of ordering, shipping, and releasing the butterflies went. With only a few days' notice, the company shipped the butterflies. They did a great job of ensuring each butterfly was protected from harm and arrived safely. So, I had individually wrapped butterflies for each guest to release at the conclusion of the memorial service, and ordered a nice decorative box of butterflies for Mason and Palmer to release.

Two women from Healing Place Church came on board and helped coordinate and organize everything. Rain was in the forecast, so we all prayed for no rain. The day before the memorial, I begged God for nice weather, and I had faith it would be clear. I knew in my heart that God would not orchestrate this large event to let it be rained out. I knew in my heart everything would fall into place.

I was still bothered that I was angry toward the emergency services staff. God really worked on my heart the weekend before the memorial service, and He gently nudged me to forgive. I remember crying out to God and begging Him to heal my heart. I had grown weary of trying to forgive. I needed closure. I could not take the battle that was going on within my heart. My heart had to forgive so that I could move forward and not let this anger and resentment turn me into a bitter and mean person. Then, God laid it on my heart that I needed to go to the fire station—the same station that responded to the call—and invite all of them to the memorial service.

I must be honest, I was not enthusiastic about what God laid on my heart to do. I even told God no. He wrestled with me, though, and I knew in my heart that He wanted me to do this. I felt God tell me this was a spiritual opportunity for these firemen to come and not only bring peace and healing, but also deliver a spiritual message that would hopefully change their lives for the better eternally.

That Monday evening, two days before the memorial service, I chickened out. I knew I needed to go, I just could not go that night. I think I even ran late at work and was relieved I did run late, so I could justify to myself that I would go the next night—the night before the memorial service.

I was nauseous and nervous all day. At some time during that day, God made me realize that the firefighters needed this as well. For the first time, I began to put myself in their shoes and see the firefighter's point of view—being thrown into a situation with a toddler was not only a firefighter's worst nightmare, but the worst nightmare for EMS as well. I knew from talking with a good friend of mine, who was a paramedic in New Orleans, that they just did not get the training they needed to work on children. At that moment, God softened my heart even further to realize that the firefighter had been struggling this past year as well.

The closer the end of the workday came, the more nervous I became. I had no earthly idea what I was going to say. My hands were sweaty, and I was shaking just going from the office to Monica's car. I asked Monica to go with me instead of Robert. I knew Robert's grief was at a different stage than mine, which is normal, and his heart was not ready to go to the fire station with me. This was something God led me to do. The entire ride to the fire station, I shook, had a rapid heartbeat, was nauseous, and kept telling Monica that I could not do it. Of course, she encouraged me and told me how proud she was of me, that I was following what God told me to do. She also kindly questioned my decision not to tell Robert what I was doing. In my heart, I knew what God was leading me to do, and I had to proceed with the plan.

It was dusk when Monica pulled up to the fire station. I let out a few loud sighs and told Monica how nervous I was and that I did not know what to say. She encouraged me and told me God was with me and that I could do this. We got out of the car, and I went up to knock on the front door. Within a few seconds, a man in uniform opened the door, and I introduced myself and he told us to come in. With my voice quivering, I told him that my name was Krista Bruns and that I was the mom of the little boy who drowned in the pond in Mallard Lakes a year ago. Before I could say another word, I saw a man walking toward me and I heard him ask, "Sutton?"

I looked to my left and realized it was the firefighter who had been the first on the scene. He had tears in his eyes as he walked toward me. We hugged and sobbed in each other's arms. He gave me the most heartfelt hug. I have no idea how long we hugged and cried together. It sounds strange to say, but I felt the pain he had been going through in his heart just from our embrace. My heart hurt for him, knowing he had been struggling like I had. Although there were no words exchanged other than him saying, "Sutton," every single ounce of bitterness I had toward him and the other firefighters immediately left my heart.

I remember he apologized and said he was sorry that he could not save Sutton. I told them the good things that had come out of Sutton's death—the large number of people who attended the service, the lives eternally changed, the addition of the Swim Strong, Jr. program by Woman's Center for Wellness, teaching special needs children under the age of five how to swim, about the things people had done in memory of Sutton like donating money to Southdown's Elementary, the best special needs preschool and Kindergarten in Baton Rouge, and donating to the Emerge Center for children with hearing and speech problems, and about how my friend Melanie, named her race horse Sutton's Smile, to keep his memory alive.

I told the firefighter that I was having a memorial service the next evening and wanted him to come. I told him everything that happened was all in God's plan. He told me that not a day went by that he did not think of Sutton and how he could not even drive by the neighborhood without thinking of him. He informed me he could not even look in the direction of our neighborhood and informed me how he used to pray and go to church, but he had not been able to do that since Sutton's death. I told him God did not want him to be tormented and that there was a higher purpose. I told him I wanted to send him a picture of Sutton smiling and wanted him to replace the image in his mind of him working on Sutton with the picture I would send him.

I got permission to text him the photo and we both agreed to delete each other's phone numbers afterwards. The firefighter agreed that he would start trying to put the good picture of Sutton smiling in his mind instead of the one and only way he ever saw Sutton. With the other two firefighters, Monica, the firefighter who worked on Sutton, and me all crying and sniffling, one of them said it is their worst nightmare to be called to a scene of a child and it could have easily been one of them. I handed them the flyer and invited them to come to the memorial service the following day.

I cried tears of joy, and my heart felt so relieved and free—every ounce of anger and resentment and bitterness for the firefighter was gone. I truly forgave him. I realized he was only doing his best and was thrown into a tragic situation that is every first responder's worst nightmare. I cried tears of sadness, knowing that he relived that tragic evening over and over every day since the night of Sutton's drowning. My heart was heavy knowing I had carried so much anger in my heart while he was suffering emotionally and spiritually. I was ashamed that I wished emotional pain on him. I immediately prayed that God would lead him back to church and that God would heal his heart and take away his pain. I cried tears of thankfulness that I learned how to truly forgive. My heart was full and overwhelmed with genuine unconditional love. The freedom that my heart felt at that moment was indescribable. It was peaceful and free from the bondage of anger that had been inside me.

Although I had forgiven the firefighter and my heart wanted everything good for him and for him to be blessed and at peace, I instantly thought of the deputy—the one who threatened to arrest the physicians at the scene if they tried to help Sutton. I thought of the cold look in his eyes and thought about how distant and disconnected he was, and for a few minutes,

I had anger towards him. I had a flash back of the firefighter's expressions—he had a look of desperation, and he was truly working so hard to resuscitate Sutton. His eyes were filled with fear, but there was a sense of compassion that I could see in his eyes during that flashback in my head. Although I relived that night in great detail over and over again, it was not until my heart had forgiven the firefighter that I saw the situation from his perspective and saw the compassion in his eyes and in his actions.

I saw a different look in the deputy's eyes. Although the sting was still in my heart when I thought of the deputy, my heart began to soften, and I became sad. I was sad because I thought about what could have happened in the deputy's life and all the things he must have witnessed in his life to become that cold. I began to pray that God would soften his heart and put the deputy on a positive spiritual journey, and change his life eternally for the better as well. Learning how to forgive the deputy from afar was even more challenging, but I was able to forgive him as well. True forgiveness set my heart completely free. It was an amazing feeling. Learning true forgiveness came with the expensive price of losing Sutton.

I have to admit that I am still struggling with forgiving the owners of the bus company for their negligence. I am better, and God is still working with me. I am a work in progress, just like we all are. My prayer is that by the time this book comes out, I can fully forgive the owners of the bus company. The sting is still there a little, but thank God, I am headed in the right direction.

I was on a spiritual high after leaving the fire station. Monica and I cried tears of joy, and we both were in awe of God's work in my heart. She had prayed that I would learn to forgive. We both said what a blessing it was that I did not go to the fire station that Monday night, because there was a huge chance that the firefighter on the scene would not have been there. My heart prevented me from going on Monday night for a reason, for we both knew that it was divine intervention that the firefighter who worked so hard to save Sutton was truly the one I was meant to meet with in person. Monica and I were both positively overwhelmed by what transpired that night.

The entire way home, I could not wait to tell my children, Robert, and my mom about how it felt to truly forgive and how the firefighter was truly sorry and how we embraced and cried together and how healing it was. After all, I did not bite my tongue in front of my family when it came to the anger I felt in my heart. I was happy that I could share how wonderful it felt to have truly forgiven. I wanted my children to see that I worked hard to follow God's plan and that true forgiveness has to be learned. I wanted to be a positive example. And, I wanted them to know that the firefighter tried his hardest, he was sorry he could not save Sutton, and we needed to pray for him to find peace.

Unfortunately, the wonderful news I had to share about meeting with the firefighter in person did not go over very well with my husband. We verbally fought, which unfortunately ended in Monica having to call the fire station and disinvite the firefighters. My heart was devastated. I felt that having the firefighters there would be a huge turning point in true forgiveness, that we would all come together for a higher purpose, and God would use the memorial service to touch the lives of the firefighters.

I do not understand why it happened the way it did. I do not have an answer. I do know that my husband is a good man, a wonderful father, and his intentions are good. In time, I know he will learn to forgive just as I have. Learning to forgive takes a lot of work, effort and a lot of time with God. My timing was different than his.

The memorial service was nothing short of a miracle. The weather was perfect. The white wooden chairs were perfectly arranged facing the front of my house, with the pond a few feet behind the last row of chairs. There was live music. Pastor Mike preached on Psalm 23, and he went verse by verse to explain it in detail, which was beautiful. Neighbors, friends, family, and co-workers came. Friends of Bennett, Palmer, and Mason came, as well as their families.

At the conclusion of the service, just before sunset, each person received a blue triangle folded paper with Sutton's birthdate and death date, and enclosed in each piece of paper was a live butterfly, along with a slip of paper containing the instructions for releasing the butterfly. Everyone was encouraged to freely walk around the six acres of land and release their butterfly. It was beautiful. Everyone was happy and full of peace and love. The moment was priceless and overwhelming.

Dinner was served and everyone had a place to sit at one of the tables on the back patio or by the pool. I hired a gentleman to play the guitar and sing while everyone ate. I must add that it stormed the day before and the day after the memorial service. It was no coincidence that the weather for the memorial service was picture-perfect.

I was in awe of how God used a tragic situation and a sweet four-year-old's life to bring so much peace and love into that evening—an evening that each of those who attended the memorial service can tell you was truly amazing and inspiring. Sweet Sutton's life would positively affect so many in an eternal way. It was at this moment that I could see the big picture and all the things that prepared me for this moment.

Chapter Five

"For I know the plans and thoughts that
I have for you," says the Lord, "plans for
peace and well-being and not for disaster,
to give you a future and a hope."

Jeremiah 29:11 AMP

SHORTLY AFTER SUTTON'S MEMORIAL SERVICE, MY
learning to forgive and the life lesson I learned was
confirmed once again in a "happenstance" meeting. Or
was it really a chance meeting?

Those who know me well know I do not believe in
coincidences. Often, when I allow doubt to creep in
my mind, I must quote my friend, Britta, and remind
myself that "there are no coincidences" in life.

On June 16, 2016, just a little over three months
after Monica and I went to the fire station and Sutton's
memorial service, my friend, Dianne Morris Rathcke,
and I left to go to Biloxi, Mississippi, for a girls' spa
weekend at the IP Casino and Spa. We planned to sleep
late, lay out by the pool, read, and go to the amazing
spa. I also planned to work on writing a few of the final

chapters for this book, something I felt God leading me to complete. Little did I know that it would bring another life changing experience and life lesson.

My original plan before leaving for Biloxi was for Dianne and me to arrive at the hotel, freshen up and change, go listen to music and drink a glass of wine. However, once Dianne and I checked in around 8:30 p.m. and settled into our room, we were both tired. We went back and forth trying to decide if we wanted to change and go downstairs to listen to music or if we wanted to turn in early. After we both agreed we wanted to just stay in the room and sleep, I brushed my teeth and flossed (of course), then was going to unpack my suitcase so I could go to sleep early. Dianne and I had to be up early the next morning for our spa day.

As soon as I finished rinsing with mouthwash, out of nowhere, I decided that since it was ladies' night in the bar, and the drinks were complimentary, we should go down and have one drink, listen to the band, and then come back to the room. I assured Dianne that we would be no longer than an hour at the most. Dianne, being the accommodating friend, agreed to go downstairs with me if I gave her time to change clothes.

I stayed in the clothes I traveled in—black yoga pants and a tank top and sandals, and looked like I was going to the gym. Dianne changed into "going out" clothes, and we headed down. As soon as we left the room, I assured her that we were not going to be long. Again, it is important once again to note what my plan was!

The lobby bar was packed—standing room only. There was a great band playing, and everyone in the bar was dressed much nicer than I was! I definitely underestimated the lobby bar on a Thursday night, but that did not prevent me from going in. The manager graciously escorted us to what appeared to be his only open booth. The two of us sat on a black leather sofa that could easily seat nine or ten people. The velvet rope in front of us kept us separated from everyone else.

A little while after we were seated, two beautiful and sweet ladies, who were much younger than we were, asked us, "Excuse me, do you ladies mind if we join you? We are in the Air Force and this is our last night here before heading home, and we are just here to hang out and not here to be hit on by guys and just want to sit and not be bothered."

Of course, Dianne and I allowed them to join us. We all introduced ourselves, and started to talk. About an hour or so later, Dianne and the other two girls got up and went to dance. When they did, I noticed a black man dressed like a cowboy. I did a double-take. I never had seen a black man dressed like a cowboy. He was wearing a huge, off-white cowboy hat about as big as the state of Texas, and cowboy boots, and his belt buckle was almost as big as his hat. I stared at him for a few minutes, watching him sitting in a black leather club chair, interacting with the group of gentlemen he was sitting with in somewhat of a circle. I laughed to myself in a respectful way, for all I could see clearly were his white teeth glowing in the dark and huge off-white cowboy hat, due to the very dim lighting in the bar. His white teeth, glowing against his jet-black skin, reminded me of the episode of *Friends* when Ross whitened his teeth and they glowed in the dark. This black cowboy had a presence about him that had the attention of every gentleman sitting around him.

I sat by myself and saw how much fun the ladies were having dancing, so I moved toward them and transferred from my wheelchair into one of the black club chairs just a few feet from our booth, to be closer to where everyone was dancing. Right after I moved, the same man with the glowing teeth and big cowboy hat passed right by me. I cannot remember how our conversation started, but I remember that I politely told him that I did not want him to be offended, but I had never seen a black cowboy before.

As soon as he spoke, I heard the most distinct southern accent I had ever heard. I laughed and picked on him in a respectful manner about his accent. I introduced myself.

I immediately asked, "Where is your Southern accent from?"

He shook my hand and replied, "My name is Pat, and I am from Georgia."

I instantly thought of the Pat character skit from NBC's *Saturday Night Live,* and I chuckled. As much of a cowboy as he looked, I did not expect him to have the name, Pat. I, of course, made a nice comment about his white teeth and told him I was a dentist and that was the first thing I noticed about people. I asked him what he was doing in Biloxi, and he told me he was in town for a firefighter's convention for the fire chiefs in his region.

Instantly, I knew that this was not a chance meeting. I laughed with God. I mean what are the odds of me being in Biloxi the last night of a fire chiefs' convention!

Because of my reaction, Pat asked me, "Do you have a problem with firefighters?"

"Not anymore, but I used to," I replied.

Intrigued by my response, Pat stayed to continue our conversation. I seized the opportunity and told him the story of Sutton, my book, and how I did not find it coincidental at all that I was supposed to work on my book that weekend and there I was sitting with a fire chief.

Pat sat down next to me and very intently listened to my story. I spared no details. It was like God made time stand still, and I was completely unaware of anything or anyone around me except this fire chief. I felt that he needed to hear what went wrong so that he could prevent this from happening in his department. I felt someone's life would be saved in the future if Pat heard what went wrong.

After a few hours of talking, Pat stood up and told me he was going to give me his business card. He told me, if he could be of any assistance in the future with helping me implement positive changes in the emergency response services in Baton Rouge, he would like to help. He told me that he taught and trained firefighters and gave lectures across his region. I looked at his name in larger bold black letters, Deron "Pat" Wilson and the word "Chief" was directly under his name. Then, as I looked at the smaller print in the lower corner to read the address, I burst out into tears. I cried so uncontrollably that the manager of the bar came over to see if I was okay and if I needed anything.

I could not control my tears and was so taken back by the address on the business card that I could not verbally tell the manager that I was okay and that Pat was not bothering me in any way. The look on Pat's face was like, "What the heck kind of crazy lady is this?" but he was kind and patient in trying to calm me down to figure out what was wrong. As he knelt beside me, I finally calmed down enough to tell him about the address of the fire station on his business card.

The address of Chief Pat's fire station was on Turkey Creek Road in Newnan, Georgia. And I lived on Turkey Creek Drive in Baton Rouge, Louisiana. That was no coincidence. I suddenly became aware that I almost did not go down to the bar that night, but I had a sudden change of plans at the last minute. Pat quickly told me he was not one to go hang out at a bar either, but he went down with his buddies at the last minute too and almost did not go.

After we both composed ourselves and talked about divine intervention, that our meeting served some higher purpose, and we were supposed to meet, we looked up and the lights were on in the bar, the bar had cleared, and the band was packing up. I had forgotten that there was even a band there. I was so engrossed in sharing my story and using it as a platform to encourage any positive change that Pat could make in the fire department so that my tragedy would not happen in his city, I was unaware of anything going on around me.

We then got on the subject about how we were both Christians and that he spoke in church sometimes and was very active in church. We shared our spouses' names and the ages of our children, and we both agreed to keep in touch. We parted ways, both of us in awe of how God orchestrated our meeting. It confirmed what I knew in my heart: there is always a reason for everything and there are no coincidences in life. We are just so caught up in the crazy world that we do not have our spiritual eyes open. We both parted knowing that we would meet again in the future. We knew there was a purpose, but did not know what was yet to come.

A few weeks later, Pat reached out to me and told me that in the future he would like me to speak and give my story at one of the fire chiefs' or firefighters' conventions. We both agreed the message had to be positive and uplifting and motivate these men and women to reflect and see if there were any positive changes he or she could make in each of their departments. We also did not want to bash anyone and wanted to make sure the message was given from both my point of view and the firefighter's point of view.

****

In August of 2016, the National Weather Service issued a flash flood warning for Baton Rouge and around twenty other parishes in South Louisiana. My area was expected to have twenty to thirty inches of rain in just twenty-four to thirty-six hours. Baton Rouge and its surrounding areas were hit hard. My family and I had to move across the street to a neighbor's house and stayed for a few days because the water started rising quickly. Cell phone service was out the majority of the time during the flood, as was the Internet. When cell phone service was restored, I received a text from Pat. He was checking on us and said he was praying for everyone. After seeing the damage on television, he asked if there was any way that his county could help. I immediately texted Pastor Mike. I told him about the story of me being in a bar and meeting Chief Pat, and how he asked if there was anything his department could do to help.

I asked for permission to put Chief Pat in touch with Pastor Mike. Pastor Mike gave us a list of supplies that the church needed immediately to aid in disaster recovery. I must say, thank God for churches. I love the fact that all the churches—it does not matter if it is Christian or Jewish and does not matter what denomination—rally together to help anyone in need during an emergency.

In just two weeks, Chief Pat, his entire fire department, and the wonderful and generous citizens of Coweta County, Georgia, gathered two truckloads of supplies to donate to Healing Place Church to aid in disaster recovery. On August 27, 2016, Chief Pat and three of his coworkers –Maria Navia, Chris Lowe, and Mark Griffin—all volunteered their time, without pay, to deliver the supplies and help assist the citizens of Baton Rouge, Denham Springs, and Prairieville.

The Coweta County Fire Department and the entire community donated more than $100,000 worth of supplies. Chief Pat told me even families who could not afford to donate were dropping supplies off at the fire station. The photos of the supplies donated in less than two weeks warmed my heart and overwhelmed me at the same time. One person makes a difference.

Healing Place Church asked that the two large truckloads of supplies be delivered to the parking lot of what was going to eventually be the Healing Place Church campus in Denham Springs. And guess who just happened to be there escorting the firefighters from Georgia in with their truckload of supplies? None other than Joe Leblanc and another member of my Bible study group at Healing Place Church. As you have already read, Joe and his wife, Dr. Cheri Leblanc, were at the hospital the night Sutton died. Joe texted me to tell me he had uncontrollable tears streaming down his face, knowing that Sutton was the reason these supplies were donated. And that chance meeting between Chief Pat and me in Biloxi, at the bar of all places, led to the generous people of Coweta County, Georgia, donating the much-needed supplies to help with cleanup. I was amazed and in awe of how God continued to use Sutton's tragedy to bless people and how God continued to remind me that He was in control, and that one little four-year-old's life does make a difference.

Before Chief Pat came to Baton Rouge, I gave him permission to tell his co-workers about Sutton's story and our meeting. I must say, there was an instant connection we all had the evening we met. During a family trip to Auburn University in October of 2016, for Bennett to tour the school since it was among his top three choices, I arranged for Chief Pat, Chris, and Mark to meet Robert and my remaining three children. Maria was invited but had to work that night. We all met up for dinner at a Mexican restaurant in Newnan, Georgia, less than an hour away from Auburn. Chris brought his wife, Jeanny, and Mark brought his fiancée, Jenny, who is also a firefighter for another county in Georgia. Chief Pat had a work meeting, but he was able to stop by for a few minutes and meet Robert and the children. We all hit it off very well, and everyone had a great evening. Chief Pat gave each of my children a beautiful coin from the Coweta County Fire Department and a Coweta County t-shirt. Of course, Palmer and

Mason loved this and were instantly fond of Chief Pat and the rest of the firefighters and their significant others. Chris and Jeanny brought their two daughters. It was an amazing evening. I sat in awe of how we were all connected and how much good could come out of Sutton's earthly death. My heart was sad, since not a day goes by that I do not miss Sutton, yet my heart was full, knowing how many people were helped by Sutton even after his death.

At dinner, I invited them all to be my guests at the Artemis Mardi Gras Soiree'—a ball for the all-female Mardi Gras Krewe in Baton Rouge, and our guests. I had just been invited to join by a friend and patient a few months prior, and I wanted each of the firefighters and their significant others to join me.

A few months after meeting everyone for dinner, I received a text from one of the firefighters, sharing a link to a news article about a missing toddler in Coweta County and how the toddler got out of the house. The article stated there were wooded areas all around. There was a huge county-wide rescue effort going on, which included so many people in the community. These firefighters texted me after the child was found safely by some people in the community and told me that they thought about Sutton and me the entire time and would not stop the search until the child was found. I think I remember seeing a photo on the news page that showed a helicopter searching as well. I cried tears of joy when I heard the child was found safely. Knowing my four firefighter friends were thinking of Sutton, a boy they never even met, and it fueled their determination to find this missing child, gave my heart even more peace. Although civilians found the boy, the fact that these four firefighters thought of Sutton made my heart full.

In January 2017, Maria, her friend, Chris, Jeanny, Mark, and Jenny all came to Baton Rouge for the Mardi Gras ball for the parade I was in. Chief Pat and his wife were unfortunately unable to come due to a work meeting. I hosted dinner at my house on Friday night. Thanks to my caterer, and with the help of Palmer and Mason, the evening was perfect. My friend, Dianne, who went to the IP with me, came to my house for dinner too.

After dinner, we all went outside on my back patio to enjoy the nice weather. We lit the fire pit and talked. Mark pulled me aside, and we started talking about the details of Sutton's tragedy and how so many things went wrong. I admitted that I had been so angry about everything that went wrong. After I spoke, Mark graciously told me that the fire department was moving toward a dual certification program that required all firefighters in Coweta County to not only be a firefighter, but they also had to get their paramedic certification— which is the highest field medical certification. Mark shared with me that he had been frustrated about not wanting to do it because he had been trained as a firefighter and had CPR certification as well as first aid.

However, after hearing all the things that went wrong the evening of Sutton's drowning, Mark tearfully told me that his heart had changed and his attitude about the required certification changed.

He told me he saw the necessity behind the training, and he was excited about getting it. I told him I would be at his graduation with bells on. Mark told me he did not want to be in a situation where he could have needed more training to save a life. I know without a doubt that Mark receiving his certification will make a positive difference in the number of lives saved due to his extra training. We will not know on earth whose life will be positively changed by Mark, but I know he will make a positive impact in this world, and he will look back and be so grateful for his training.

My goal is to have every city require this dual certification and to have more training—more hands-on training and more medical mock drills. Not every city requires this dual certification, but they should. I am so proud of the Coweta County Fire/Rescue department. Lives in this town will be forever changed for the good—even if only one life is saved, it is worth it. Every life matters. Every life makes a difference!

The evening after our dinner and talk on the patio, we all stayed downtown in Baton Rouge and went to the black-tie ball. The evening was phenomenal. We stayed up late, dancing to the live band, hanging out, and having fun. The morning after the ball, we all met for brunch before my Georgia friends had to leave. We said our goodbyes, and Mark and Jenny invited us to their wedding.

I have become very fond of those four firefighters, and I know we were all placed in each other's lives for a reason. Although I have only had a few encounters with them, I have a deep spiritual bond with them that cannot be explained. I love each of them deeply, and I am so happy for my divine meeting.

On March 2, 2017, exactly two years since Sutton went to Heaven, the connection to these Georgia firefighters deepened when they texted me, telling me that one of the firefighters in Coweta County passed away. The news articles reported it as the first in-the-line-of-duty death in Coweta County. A chance meeting on June 16, 2016? Absolutely no way! There are no coincidences. I believe in my heart that even though Sutton and this firefighter who died did not know me or my family, Sutton ran to greet him in Heaven. I believe that is how interconnected we are.

Chapter Six

"But those who wait for the Lord [who expect, look for, and hope in Him] will gain new strength and renew their power; They will lift up their wings [and rise up close to God] like eagles [rising toward the sun]; They will run and not become weary; They will walk and not grow tired."

Isaiah 40:31AMP

PEOPLE MIGHT WONDER HOW I AM ABLE TO GET out of bed every morning after experiencing such a heartbreaking loss. Most are curious why I am not angry with God and ask me how my faith in God is so strong. It is only when I reflect back to my childhood and give the details of my life that one can know how I can even make it through the day and see how I live beneath the surface of what one's earthly eyes see.

So many people bury their feelings and put a mask on and hide from what is truly on the inside. Including myself, no one wants to talk about how they truly feel for fear of rejection and judgement. We all hide what is on the inside. However, beneath the surface, we truly are all the same.

My prayer is that no matter what someone has been through in life and no matter how alone or miserable or sad or broken they feel right now, by the end of reading this book, my story will be one of hope, bring peace, and show that each of our lives has meaning and purpose. I want people to know that they are not alone, and I want to help restore inner joy. My circumstances are different, but I know first-hand the pain and suffering this world brings.

I grew up in the Park Forest neighborhood in Baton Rouge, Louisiana. Park Forest was a middle- to upper-middle-class neighborhood and had an elementary and middle school, a Baptist church, a Methodist church, a neighborhood grocery store, a neighborhood pool, and a snowball stand. Most moms in the neighborhood were either stay-at-home moms, teachers, or worked part-time. There was a sense of community and support for one another and a sense of genuine caring for neighbors.

My mom, dad, and my older sister, Tammy, and I lived next to a retired couple whom many of the kids on my street, including my sister and me, called "Paw-Paw Sam" and "Maw-Maw Murt" Robinson, even though they were not related to anyone on the street. They treated all the neighborhood kids as if we were their own grandchildren. Paw-Paw Sam bought me my first ice cream cone from the ice cream truck that would come through the neighborhood. Looking back, I now realize how fortunate I was to grow up in such a wonderful neighborhood that was safe to live in, and in a time that was so different than the crazy world we live in today.

I grew up in an environment that is almost unheard of today, where as long as we stayed within the neighborhood and did not go past the major streets that bordered it, almost all the parents allowed their kids to roam freely. Everyone's parents, including mine, had one major rule: we had to be inside by the time the street lights were fully on. Once the street light started to flicker on, we all knew we had only a few minutes to either run home or hop on our bikes and ride as fast as we could, and be inside the house with the door shut before the street light was fully on. Many parents would walk over almost every night to the Robinsons' house and have coffee outside on Maw-Maw Murt and Paw-Paw Sam's large metal swing. Life as a child for me was almost perfect.

When I was in second grade, the Leblanc family moved into the house directly behind me. I immediately developed a great friendship with Lyle, who was the same age as me. Lyle was extremely intelligent and friendly, and we both attended Park Forest Elementary school together for a few years. Lyle and I started piano lessons around the same time; we both liked to ride bikes, skate, play outside, set up tents in the yard, play board games and play on the rope swing that hung from a huge tree in Lyle's yard. We talked about everything. He was truly my best friend. We were like two peas in a pod. Besides hanging out with Lyle, my favorite childhood memories are spending time on my grandparents' ninety-acre farm in St. Tammany Parish, and fishing with my grandfather in one of his large ponds.

My dad was an engineer for Exxon, and Mom was an elementary school guidance counselor at Park Forest Elementary. My Aunt Janeese, "Eece" I called her, was the librarian at the same school where Mom worked. My parents truly loved and cherished each other and always put my sister and me first.

I was a socially awkward child, and I liked talking with adults over the majority of children my age. I never really liked small talk and still to this day do not like small talk. I enjoy getting to the center or core of a person and truly getting to know them and understand them. Besides being relentlessly made fun of in middle school and some in the early years of high school, I really had an amazing childhood. However, I can look back and am grateful for being picked on, for it made me stronger and tougher, and it honestly helped prepare me for my life's storms.

My parents started taking me to church when I was six months old. I grew up attending Park Forest Baptist Church. Every time the church doors opened, my parents had me in church. I went to Wednesday night church, Sunday school, Sunday morning church, Sunday evening church, choir practice, Vacation Bible

School, church camp, GA's (a Bible study and mission based group for young girls), and last but not least, I was in Bible Drill. Bible Drill is when children memorize hundreds of scriptures in the Bible and have a competition each year on who can quote the scriptures word for word from the Bible when given the book of the Bible, chapter and verses.

When I was under the age of twelve, I loved going to church, but as I got older, there were times that I did not want to go, but my parents made me attend. During my middle school and high school years, I went through periods of wanting to go to church and not wanting to attend. However, it did not matter how I felt, my parents still made me attend. I remember as far back as being three or four years old and knew in my heart that there was a God, and I truly believed in God and in Jesus, not because someone told me to believe, but because in my heart, I just knew it and felt it. I knew at a very early age that each person has a purpose in life and that God made each of us, and knew in my heart that we each have a destiny to fulfill. I made a conscious decision when I was nine years old to become a Christian and get baptized. I knew in my heart that this was the right choice for me.

I must say that although I believed in God and Jesus, finding God and Jesus in church was often difficult and still can be difficult, because it was hard to find Jesus in church when there were so many judgmental people and when there were kids in church standing up singing about Jesus but making fun of me or others. However, I quickly realized and understood that my attending church was to help me grow closer to God and I needed to go. I truly knew that no one was perfect, and that included me realizing I was not perfect, and that my personal spiritual growth was hindered if I did not attend church regularly. To this day, I have to remind myself that I do not go to church for anyone else but me and my children. I need to continue to grow spiritually, for spiritual growth is a long process and a long journey and is different for each person. I am not called to like everyone I go to church with and vice versa. However, I am called to love everyone and show God's love.

Although I briefly fought with my parents on and off over the years when they forced me to go to church when I did not want to, I am now forever grateful to them that they did indeed force me to go. I am also grateful that in the middle of my eighth-grade year, my parents granted my wishes and switched me to a private Christian school, Parkview Baptist School. So, on top of being at church, I had Bible classes and chapel in school. Little did I know at the time how much I would need God and how critical my parents' decision to raise me in a Christian home and send me to a Christian school was until now. That one decision my parents made to raise me in a Christian home would impact my life for eternity. It saddens me that God has been taken out of our public schools. For without God, my life and my heart would not be the same.

Now that I am an adult and look back on my life's storms, I truly understand Proverbs 22:6, NKJV: "Train up a child in the way he should go, and when he is old, he will not depart from it."

I lived a very sheltered life. I think ours was the only house in the neighborhood that did not have a satellite dish or cable television. From kindergarten through fourth grade, I attended Park Forest Elementary where my mom worked. I loved the teachers there, and I loved the fact that I attended the same school as the kids in my neighborhood. Like any teacher's child would say, it was hard being the child of a teacher because everyone in the school and neighborhood knew my mother, which meant that everyone told my mom everything I did and said. If I coughed, my mom knew. If I got in trouble for talking in class, it felt like everyone could not wait to run to my mom and tell on me. In other words, I knew better than to do anything wrong because my mom would find out.

I think the "worst" thing I did as a teenager was lie to my parents that I went to the high school football games, and instead went to 2010 (sorry, Mom), a teen dance club, with my friends. My friends and I would call the local radio station to find out the score of the game before going home. At the time, it was very frustrating to know that some people found true pleasure in trying to do anything they could to run to my mom and tell her anything I did that was "wrong." However, looking back, this really helped me in life and kept me out of trouble. The fact that I did not want to get in trouble or disappoint my parents kept me on track to be what society would perceive as a "good" child. However, the down side was that it contributed to my extreme desire to be "perfect," and to try to please everyone, including my parents. This contributed to my desire not to be a disappointment to my parents and to be a high achiever. As an adult, it did take me quite a long time to learn to love myself, mistakes and all.

When I was seven years old, I started having horrible leg cramps. I would wake up in the middle of the night, crying because of muscle cramps in my legs. My parents kept taking me to the doctor, and every doctor kept telling them that I had growing pains and to soak my legs in Epsom salts. I then started to walk funny. Whether people knew me or not, people would either come up to my parents or come up to me and ask what was wrong with me. This began my life-long battle of people asking what was wrong with me and always pointing out that something was wrong with me.

Luckily, my parents, sister, grandparents, teachers, close neighbors and true friends protected me from people like this. I was fortunate that my close family and friends and positive people in my life treated me very well and respected me as a "normal" child and saw past my physical limitations. Because of how amazing my parents, sister, neighbors, teachers, pastors and close friends were, even as a young child, I knew that although there was something wrong with me physically, this did not change who I was as a person. I was loved and had a purpose in life, and God had a plan for me. Looking back, I was grateful that I learned this at an early age, for there are many people who never realize this.

My parents took me to several different doctors for many years before my mom finally found Dr. Charles Tessier, who was fresh out of medical school. He ordered a blood test to check my muscle enzymes. When the test came back abnormal, Dr. Tessier sent me to Children's Hospital in New Orleans. I was diagnosed at nine years old with a neuromuscular disorder affecting my legs. Thankfully, it did not affect my heart or lungs. I had numerous foot surgeries and years of physical therapy. I am thankful that my family, teachers, and close friends treated me like they would any other person. They did not allow me to feel sorry for myself and all had high expectations of me and for me. My parents did a great job of not holding me back and taught me that my mind was great and not to let anyone or anything, including a physical disability, stand in my way, and to always seek God's will for my life.

One time in middle school, I came home and told my parents I wanted to try out for the girls' middle school basketball team. I have no idea why, because I do not like basketball, but I thought I could and would make the team. My parents encouraged me to try out if that was what I wanted. Although my little bird legs could barely run, I really thought I would make the team. After practicing after school for a week or so with all of the girls trying to make the team, I was shocked when I did not make the team. Looking back, I can see why I did not make it. I was really horrible at sports. However, I credit my parents and teachers for teaching me not to let anything stop me. Again, this prepared me for what was yet to come.

Each disappointment, each failure, each surgery, each person who crossed my path, and whatever challenges I was faced with at this young age were all meant to prepare me, emotionally and spiritually, for what was yet to come. I am forever grateful to my parents, friends, family, teachers, doctors and other people God placed in my life. Each of you helped prepare me for what was yet to come.

Chapter Seven

"Through Him we also have access by faith into this [remarkable state of] grace in which we [firmly and safely and securely] stand. Let us rejoice in our hope and the confident assurance of [experiencing and enjoying] the glory of [our great] God [the manifestation of His excellence and power]. And not only this, but [with joy] let us exult in our sufferings and rejoice in our hardships, knowing that hardship (distress, pressure, trouble) produces patient endurance; and endurance, proven character (spiritual maturity); and proven character, hope and confident assurance [of eternal salvation]. Such hope [in God's promises] never disappoints us, because God's love has been abundantly poured out within our hearts through the Holy Spirit who was given to us."   Romans 5:2-5 AMP

"Consider it nothing but joy, my brothers and sisters, whenever you fall into various trials. Be assured that the testing of your faith [through experience] produces endurance [leading to spiritual maturity, and inner peace]. And let endurance have its perfect result and do a thorough work, so that you may be perfect and completely developed [in your faith], lacking in nothing."   James 1:2-4 AMP

I MET ROBERT, MY HUSBAND, WHEN I WAS SIXTEEN years old. He was seventeen. Robert and I married July 24, 1993. He started dental school in the fall of 1995 at Louisiana State University School of Dentistry, and I went on to graduate from Southeastern Louisiana University in December of 1995. I graduated with a B.S. in pre-professional biology, with a minor in chemistry. I started dental school in New Orleans in the fall of 1998. I found out at the medical screening for dental school that I was pregnant. My due date was in November around Thanksgiving break, so I in no way had any concerns with missing school. Christmas break was right around the corner from Thanksgiving; therefore, everything in my mind would work out smoothly.

I decided not to tell any teachers nor students nor administration at the dental school that I was pregnant until the after I signed all of my papers, my tuition was received, and orientation was over. I did not want them to kick me out. I knew they legally could not, but I wanted to make sure. Like medical school, the first year of dental school is the hardest. The number of classes and the large amount of reading and studying is extremely intense. There were many nights of just a few hours of sleep, and some sleepless nights, due to the amount of studying involved. So, it was no surprise to me that I freaked everyone out my first day of dental school when I informed the administration and professors I was pregnant. I believe I was the first person to start the first year of dental school pregnant.

For my protection and the baby's protection, the dental school administration had me wear a gas mask and special gloves during Gross Anatomy. My classmates were incredible and were very supportive of me. Just about a month-and-a-half into my first year of dental school, I ended up prematurely bleeding due to placenta previa, and I had to be rushed to East Jefferson General Hospital in Metairie in the middle of a school night. I ended up almost bleeding to death, had several blood transfusions, and an emergency C-section performed by a doctor in Metairie. My regular OB-GYN, Dr. Sharon Lee, was in Baton Rouge and I could not make it there in time since I was bleeding so much. A team of doctors (two OB-GYNs, an anesthesiologist, and a neonatal intensive care physician) from East Jefferson General Hospital came into my room before taking me to surgery and told me, in front of Robert and my parents, that I had lost so much blood that it was highly probable that either the baby or I or both would not make it. The lead OB-GYN told me that he had a patient who bled to death before they could get her up to surgery.

I planned my funeral for the first time, verbally, right there in the hospital room. I told Robert I wanted a live band and he better not have my funeral in a funeral home—I wanted a church, and I requested a slide show with photos showing me living life and having fun. There was no time for an epidural—the anesthesiologist had to use general anesthesia. I remember the nitrous mask going on my nose, and I remember thinking I was going to die and go to Heaven that night. I knew Bennett would make it. I was at peace knowing I was going to die. As long as my baby lived, I was happy and at peace. I woke up from anesthesia and immediately was upset when I realized I had not died, because I knew the chances of us both making it were slim. Thank You, Jesus, I was immediately told that we both made it.

On September 23, 1998 at 4:40 a.m., Bennett Alexander Bruns came into this world eight weeks premature. I knew at that moment that God had big plans for Bennett and God was not finished with me yet. Bennett was in NICU for six weeks. He was on a ventilator and had blood transfusions and an IV in his head. Two days after he was born, Hurricane George approached and New Orleans was evacuated. This was supposed to be the hurricane that wiped out New Orleans.

I was basically kicked out of the hospital since I was well enough to go home, even though my baby was in NICU. The hospital needed the beds in preparation for the hurricane. I tried to get Bennett moved to Woman's Hospital in Baton Rouge via ambulance, but the doctors said it was too risky to move him. Robert and I lived in a flood zone in Metairie, and the hotel rooms were all booked. The hospital would not let us stay in the waiting room and sleep on the floor, so our only option was to either stay on the second floor of our townhome and pray we would be okay or pack up and head to Baton Rouge and stay with my parents. I was hysterical—I could not believe I was told to evacuate, yet I was expected to leave my baby behind in the hospital.

The doctors, my parents, and Robert all told me we were no good to our baby if we stayed and died in the hurricane, and they begged me to go to Baton Rouge. The doctors and nurses at the hospital assured me the hospital had generators, was well built, and the NICU was well protected. I reluctantly went to the townhouse with Robert, helped him carry our things upstairs, packed our car, got our cat, and got in the car for him to drive to Baton Rouge. All of this after I had just had an emergency C-section and blood transfusion, along with studying for school. I dozed off in the car and kept hearing Bennett crying—it was really the cat meowing—but in the fog my brain was in, I thought it was Bennett. I felt like a horrible mother for packing up the cat but having to leave my premature baby behind in the hospital. I had hate in my heart towards the hospital administration and doctors for discharging me from the hospital during a hurricane.

We stayed in Baton Rouge with my parents. The nurses and doctors at EJGH in Metairie were so good about calling us and keeping us updated. The hurricane ended up affecting Baton Rouge and sparing New Orleans. As soon as the roads opened, Robert sped down River Road to the hospital. Due to the hurricane, I technically only missed two days of dental school. Once school resumed, I stayed in school, and Robert and I went to visit Bennett almost every evening during visitation for six weeks. Robert was in his fourth year of dental school, and I was in my first year. We went to school Monday through Friday all day and went to visit Bennett almost every evening after school and on the weekends. We did miss a day or two here and there if we had big tests, but I knew I had to stay in school and complete school.

The day Bennett came home from the hospital, I had a huge test. In dental school, if you missed a test, the make-up test was so difficult that it was almost impossible to pass. So, my parents drove in and went with Robert to take Bennett home from NICU. Robert was wheeled out of the maternity ward holding Bennett. I think he was the first man to be wheeled out of the maternity ward. I have a photo of Robert in the wheelchair with the nurses and transporter laughing in the background—all in good fun.

I was the first person in the history of the dental school to start dental school pregnant and graduate on time four years later. Little did I know that what I had just gone through would make me even stronger. Again, this prepared me for what was yet to come.

Bennett was a miracle baby, and I felt God's presence the entire time. Since Bennett's birth in 1998, Palmer was born five weeks early in 2004, Mason was born in 2005, and Sutton was born several weeks premature in 2010.

When I was seven months pregnant with Mason, my weak legs gave out one day, while I was walking. My left knee buckled, and I just sat down on my left ankle and broke my left leg and ankle. I had emergency surgery a week later to repair my left leg and ankle. Ultimately, I ended up in a wheelchair when my legs got weaker. I did not let this stop me. I work full-time as a dentist just fine, and I play the piano just fine using my right foot, but my legs are too weak to walk. For a very long time, I despised going anywhere in town—so many people in public who did not even know me were so mean and nosy and ugly to me and treated me differently just because I was in a wheelchair. People stared and would run up to me and ask, "What is wrong?" and "What happened?" with no regard for my privacy. Some people were genuinely nice, but most were just nosy—wanted to get "the scoop" and make themselves feel better about themselves.

People not seeing beneath my surface really bothered me. I allowed them to cripple my self-esteem. I hated going places. I became a bit of a hermit—I went out but only to places that were comfortable and familiar, and I did not deviate from my normal and safe places—safe meaning very few strangers.

Why did I care so much what other people thought? The answer is that the enemy likes to get in our minds and cripple them, make us feel less-than and feel badly about ourselves, so that we will be so focused on what others think that we will not accomplish the calling that God has on our lives!

Over time, with the help of friends, co-workers, and a lot of books, sermons, and devotionals, I finally learned to love myself—wheelchair and all. I stopped worrying about what strangers or even people I knew thought or said. God's opinion of me is the only opinion that matters. I feel so free now. I feel like a huge weight is lifted off my shoulders, and I love life and enjoy life so much. Now, if someone stops me and is rude to me or treats me like I am ignorant or talks slowly to me because I am in a wheelchair, I am kind, but I just let it roll off and honestly do not let it bother me. I have learned how to take life's obstacles and grow from them.

Chapter Eight

"Peace I leave with you; My [perfect] peace I give to you; not as the world gives do I give to you. Do not let your heart be troubled, nor let it be afraid. [Let My perfect peace calm you in every circumstance and give you courage and strength for every challenge.]"   John 14:27 AMP

WHEN I WAS TWENTY-FOUR YEARS OLD, MY mother was diagnosed with breast cancer. My mom's cancer diagnosis made me realize, for the first time in my life, that she was not invincible and would not live forever. Although I was an adult, I still thought my parents would live forever. Yes, it sounds silly—I knew we all had to die, but I was still young, naïve, and unrealistic. However, my mom's diagnosis was devastating. I remember crying, and being angry, shocked, and feeling helpless. I questioned God for a little while. My mom was a Christian, she was a great mother, and she was kind, generous and always saw the good in everyone. So, I asked God over and over again why she had to get cancer.

Between my dad's death in 2007, the five miscarriages that occurred between Mason and Sutton, and my mom's breast cancer diagnosis in January 1997, Mom's cancer was a difficult issue I have had to deal with in my life. Now that I have lost Sutton, I can look back and see that God used my mom's cancer as a baby step to prepare me for what was yet to come. It is easy to look back and reflect and see how God used my mom's diagnosis for good. Of course, I could not see it at the time she was diagnosed.

Because of my mom's cancer diagnosis, my doctor ordered mammograms for me starting at the age of thirty-five. The very first mammogram I had, the radiology technician called me back for more films of my left breast. My doctor ordered an ultrasound-guided biopsy performed by a well-respected radiologist I used to work for in college. Both my mom and dad went with me to the biopsy. Because work was so busy, Robert could not come. I was in complete shock that my first mammogram led to a biopsy of my breast. The several days I had to wait between my biopsy and the report were torture. I honestly think having my toenails ripped off would have been less painful than the wait to obtain the results.

Thank God, the results were normal. Every year following my biopsy, my doctor ordered a mammogram, and every year, I was diligent about making sure I went for my annual check-up and mammogram.

My annual mammograms were always around November—my birthday month. I was pregnant with Sutton in November 2010 and decided to wait until after my delivery to have my mammogram, since I knew having a mammogram in my third trimester would not be very comfortable. Sutton was born on December 18, 2010. That next April, I had my fourth mammogram. I remember the day well. The waiting room was busy, and the technicians were running over an hour behind. Across the waiting room, I recognized Molly, a friend from high school who was also my patient. While waiting for the tech to call us back, Molly and I talked. A few days later, the radiology technician called me back for more films because they saw a possible nodule. Luckily, the additional film proved that I did not have nodules. These areas of radiopacity (areas of white on a radiograph) were small droplets of silicone where my breast implant was starting to leak.

A year later, I started having a little pain on my left breast. I palpated my left breast but felt no lumps. I dismissed the pain and thought it was just muscular soreness from picking up Sutton. I ignored it. In April 2012, Molly came in for her six-month cleaning appointment. Before I could even say "hello," the first words out of her mouth were that she missed having me to talk to at her yearly mammogram appointment. I told Molly that she was mistaken and informed her that our yearly mammogram appointment was not until August. Molly politely informed me that we had our mammogram in April 2011, informed me that I was past due, and firmly told me not to forget to make my appointment for my mammogram.

At the end of the day, I called my doctor's office and talked to the nurse to schedule an appointment for my mammogram. However, it was too late in the day, and their office was closed. I called again the next morning to verify my mammogram date. Molly was correct. I was indeed past due for my mammogram. The nurse scheduled an appointment for me, and the mammogram date would force me to come back a day early from vacation with my family, but it was the earliest date available that coordinated with my schedule.

On May 24th, 2012, Robert, my four children, my mother, and I left to go Branson, Missouri, for vacation. Before he passed away, my father wanted to take my mom to Branson. Robert desperately wanted to take my mom to Branson as a tribute to my dad before she got to the point in life where she couldn't or wouldn't travel.

Since my mammogram appointment was that Friday, we left Branson on Thursday to start heading back to Baton Rouge. Robert decided it was best for us to spend the night in Shreveport, Louisiana, since it would only be about a four-hour drive to make it to my appointment. Before going to bed, I set my alarm and called the front desk for a wake-up call.

The next morning, my alarm went off as set, and the front desk clerk at the hotel called as requested. From what I recall, I hit the snooze button on my alarm over four times. For those who know me well, I am not a morning person and am very difficult to wake up. I sat up in the bed and told Robert that I wanted to sleep late, told him I regretted making my appointment on our last day of vacation, and told him that I would call to reschedule my mammogram for another date. I lay back down with hopes of going back to sleep. My head hit the pillow, as I was very much looking forward to going back to sleep. Within less than one minute of putting my head back on the pillow, I had this strong voice in my head saying, "Get up." Of course, I ignored this little voice.

Something in my head and heart insisted that I get up and go to my mammogram appointment. I tried to ignore the voice many times. I tried so hard to go back to sleep, but I could not go back to sleep. When the alarm went off again, Robert said, "Can't you just reschedule?" Like any great husband and father would do, he had driven the entire vacation and made sure we saw everything we wanted. He was tired from the driving and wanted to sleep late just like I did.

"Robert, I just cannot shake this gut instinct of something telling me to go to my appointment," I said. "I feel like I really need to go and not procrastinate this appointment."

Robert immediately leaped out of bed and said, "Let's go," and started getting dressed.

Looking back, there is absolutely no doubt in my mind that this voice was really God's voice, telling me to me get up and go. Robert and I frantically woke everyone up. We got all four children dressed, packed up, and ate breakfast quickly.

Since we had a late start, Robert had to go ten miles per hour over the speed limit to get me to my mammogram appointment in time. Of course, he was pulled over for speeding and received a speeding ticket. It seemed like it took the state trooper twenty minutes to verify our insurance, evaluate our registration, and write the ticket. The entire time we were waiting for the ticket, I just stared at the clock in the car. The strong need to make it to my appointment grew and grew. At this point, I knew my mammogram would not be normal. Call me crazy if you want, but I have learned from life experiences when I have had these strong feelings before. There have only been a few times I have been wrong. I called the mammogram department and informed them that I was en route and would be late, but I assured them that I would be at my appointment. The ticket did not keep Robert from speeding. He knew that it was important to me to get me to my appointment.

Of course, nothing went smoothly on our journey to get back home to Baton Rouge. The kids were hungry, everyone had to go to the restroom, and Sutton's diaper needed to be changed, so we stopped and ate barbecue in Baton Rouge. I think it was the fastest we have ever eaten. We loaded up all seven of us in the car and headed toward Woman's Hospital. Robert dropped me off in the front of the physician's tower. We looked like a NASCAR pit crew, pulling up fast and getting me out of the car. Looking back, it was a complete miracle from God that we arrived only a few minutes late for my appointment.

The nurse practitioner at my doctor's office evaluated me before my mammogram. I explained to her that I had a little pain in my left breast and showed her where the pain was. She said everything felt fine on the left side. Words cannot describe how relieved I was. For a second, I was mad at myself for not sleeping in on our last morning of our vacation. Then, she examined my right breast. She stopped around the two o'clock position on my right breast and said, "I do feel something here." My heart sank a little, and I could not help thinking of the alarm clock incident earlier that morning, and how odd it was that I had that strong instinct to not sleep late.

After my examination, I went down the elevator to have my mammogram. I asked the radiology technician what radiologist was working that day. She informed me Dr. Robert Burris was working. I told her I used to work in the radiology department with him when I was in college and babysat for him and his wife. I asked the tech to let him know that I wanted to say hello if he had time, since I had not seen him in over seventeen years.

After the tech had taken all of my digital images, she informed me that she would show the radiologist the images before I could get dressed. I sat in the room for what seemed like thirty minutes or longer. The longer the radiology technician was gone, the more anxious I became.

There was a knock on the door. The door opened and in walked the radiologist I used to babysit for. Thinking he was coming in to say hello, I was not prepared for the news he was about to tell me:

"Well, kiddo, I think this is the real deal."

I did not understand what he was trying to tell me. I do not remember what I said back to him, if anything. I was in shock once it sank into my head what Dr. Burris was telling me.

He then informed me that I needed an ultrasound of my breast and said he wanted to stay and perform the ultrasound immediately. As I rounded the corner headed to the ultrasound room, the nurse practitioner was there. She gave me this sweet smile and came over and gave me this big hug and assured me that, "We have this." She assured me that she was there for me if I needed her. Somehow, I knew I would be all right and would get through this. It was well past 4:30 p.m. when the doctor started the ultrasound. I lay down on the table next to the ultrasound machine and was in a daze.

I tried to keep my happy face on since I was usually good at doing so, but it was hard. At the same time, however, I was still shocked and kept thinking, "This cannot be happening to me." When my ultrasound was completed, Dr. Burris told me I needed a CT needle-guided biopsy and wanted me to see a breast surgeon. He was able to get in touch with one of his business partners, Dr. Steven Sotile, another radiologist I worked for in college. Thankfully, there was an opening on Monday to have the biopsy performed.

My dear friend, Monica, was waiting for me along with her daughter when I left the hospital. When I arranged for Monica to pick me up, I told her I would only be an hour to an hour-and-a-half at most. Monica waited for over three hours for me. I did not talk much on the way home, and I tried to talk in a way that her daughter would not overhear. I decided that I was not going to tell my children or my mother or anyone outside of my "inner circle" of friends about my mammogram results. I wanted to wait until the results came back. I am thankful that Robert agreed with me and honored my wishes.

My outlook was positive, and I really was not worried at that time. However, after the kids went to bed, I locked my bedroom door and went into the bathroom to take a hot bath and soak in the tub. My mind wandered as I tried to grasp what I had just been told. How could I be thirty-nine years old and have cancer? Out of the blue, I just burst into tears.

The shock of hearing those words and hearing the dreaded C word—cancer—finally wore off, and I just sobbed. I am tough—nothing much gets me down. I do not cry often. However, I sobbed and sobbed. I cried to the point that I lost my breath. After twenty minutes, I was done crying. I decided that this was the last time I was going to cry and told myself that I would get through it. God was with me, and that was all that mattered. I put my happy face on, and I felt like myself again. Of course, I was still worried, but I refused to have a pity party.

At this moment, I realized everything I went through in my life prepared me to be diagnosed with cancer. My mind flashed back to the day I heard the news about my mom having breast cancer. I remember how strong she was and how she kept a positive attitude and trusted God the entire time. I realized I was strong enough just like my mom to handle the diagnosis. Instead of each life storm dragging me down, I fought to use moments of crisis to make me stronger and learn from each experience. Although I may have been knocked down for a while, I always got back up. For me, it was imperative that I self-reflected throughout my life so I could see the lessons I was supposed to learn from my trials. By doing so, the "big picture" became much clearer to me.

I had the CT guided needle biopsy. I was so nervous for the procedure, yet it felt very surreal. The biopsy was not painful and felt like a mammogram would feel. I trusted Dr. Sotile and knew he was an excellent radiologist, so it was easy for me to relax knowing I was in good hands. I knew what the procedure was and how it was performed, but I was nervous about the outcome and nervous about having to wait for the pathology report. Waiting for the report was torture for me. The entire time I was on the table, I tried to be hopeful that I did not have cancer, but deep down in my soul, I knew I had cancer. I could see why that still small voice, on the last day of vacation, told me to get up and go to my appointment. I prayed to God and tried to remain positive.

Waiting for the results was the hard part. I remember the breast surgeon telling me the results came back as ductal carcinoma in situ (DCIS) and how my cancer was caught very early. DCIS is known as Stage 0 breast cancer—basically, if I had to have breast cancer, this was the easiest cancer to treat. The doctor made an appointment for me to see a breast surgeon. I was very fortunate to have this early diagnosis and thanked and praised God for the great news. I decided it was best for me to continue to protect my privacy and not share this with anyone other than Robert, Britta, Monica, and my co-workers.

One thing I learned from my dad's death was that I could not use people or things, like a bigger house or a nicer car or fancier clothes, to fill the pain that was going on in my heart. I had to rely on God to carry me. Although God places people in our lives to help us, I relied too much on people to comfort me after my dad died, rather than rely more on God. Like many pastors and evangelists preach, no person can be Jesus to me. Only Jesus can be Jesus to me. I had to rely on God.

Also, I did not want my young children knowing I had cancer and all of their sweet friends at school asking my children if their "mommy is going to die." I wanted my children to have as close to a normal childhood as possible and not have to worry about me. I had a dental practice to run, and I did not want my patients to avoid calling me for an emergency toothache for fear that they would bother me.

I loved my mom, but I did not want to burden her with worry. I did not want her telling her friends or other family members. I just wanted to keep everything as normal for me as possible. I did not want pity. I did not want negativity from the outside world. I just wanted to deal with my diagnosis on my own and rely on God. Going through my dad's death and having five miscarriages was far worse on me than having cancer. I had been through so much in my life already that this was just a little speedbump in the road. I knew God had given me the peace and strength to face tougher challenges, and I was confident I had the strength to get through this life storm and come out even stronger than I already was.

My mom was seventy-eight years old at the time of this writing, and she had been cancer-free for twenty years. Looking back, I could see that it was all in God's perfect plan that she was diagnosed with breast cancer.

Had my mom not had breast cancer, my doctor would not have ordered my mammograms at the age of thirty-five, and my cancer would not have been detected as early. I very likely would not have made it. I learned important life lessons and grew emotionally and spiritually because of my mom going through cancer. I watched my mom fight cancer with grace, prayers, faith, and a positive attitude. I watched her as she trusted God. The way she battled cancer helped prepare me for my battle with cancer.

Chapter Nine

"I can do all things [which He has called me
to do] through Him who strengthens and
empowers me [to fulfill His purpose—I am
self-sufficient in Christ's sufficiency; I am
ready for anything and equal to anything
through Him who infuses me with inner
strength and confident peace.]"

Philippians 4:13 AMP

I MET WITH A BREAST SURGEON WHO HAD A GREAT
reputation in Baton Rouge. David, my longtime
co-worker and friend, brought me to the appointment
and waited patiently in the waiting room. Robert had
to work, so David came with me. Because he had lost
his mother to cancer years ago, I am quite sure it
brought back painful memories of bringing her to her
appointments. Yet, it helped me knowing that he knew
what I was going through and was strong for me. Upon
checking in at the surgeon's office, I almost left. The
girl at the receptionist desk acted like she was doing
me a favor by checking me in and made it very clear to

me, and to her co-workers, that it was almost time for her lunch. She then proceeded to make sure everyone heard that, "It's hotter than a hooker in fishnets outside." I wanted to curse her out so badly and give her a piece of my mind, but I just laughed on the inside, and smiled. However, looking back, I can see that the attitude of the girl working at the front desk left me with a very unsettling feeling in my heart and gut that this was not the right office for me. However, I knew the surgeon had a wonderful reputation. So, I decided to stay for the appointment.

The breast surgeon was super nice and thorough. The surgeon explained my options—a lumpectomy or a mastectomy and went over the pros and cons of each. A lumpectomy was recommended first. If I had a lumpectomy, I could always have a mastectomy later. However, once I had a mastectomy, there was no turning back.

Although my gut instinct told me I should proceed with the mastectomy, I chose the lumpectomy. I asked about a sentinel node biopsy, and the surgeon went over the pros and cons and informed me with DCIS, there was no need to test my lymph nodes. I was very confident in the doctor, and the bedside manner was great. We decided to get an oncologist on board since my mother had a history of breast cancer and since I was only thirty-nine years old.

I did not have to bother finding an oncologist because I already knew who I was going to use. Since Britta's husband, Jeff, was diagnosed with cancer a few years prior to me being diagnosed, I chose to use his well-known and well-respected oncologist, Dr. Michael Castine. I met with Dr. Castine, and we discussed my options. I was relieved when he told me that with DCIS, I did not need chemo or radiation, unless the pathology report showed otherwise.

Shortly after meeting with the oncologist, I had a lumpectomy on my right breast. The team took excellent care of me. I thankfully had no pain at all. I was a little sore, but nothing compared to having four C-sections and multiple foot surgeries as a child and adult. The procedure was an out-patient procedure. I was back at work just a few days later. My surgeon was going out of town the day after my lumpectomy and did tell me when I made the appointment for the lumpectomy that another partner in the office would be available if I needed anything or had any complications. I was also informed I could get the results from the other partner. Basically, we needed clean margins all the way around the biopsy. If the margins were not clear, it would require more surgery.

Waiting on the results was more brutal and more stressful than waiting for the CT needle-biopsy results. I was hopeful the margins were clear, but I always prepare for the worst and hope and pray for the best. Maybe not the best attitude, but I like to be prepared. I am trying to learn to always expect the best and then deal with the worst when and if faced with it. However,

I am a work in progress, so this is a challenge I need to work on.

After waiting the necessary number of days for the biopsy results, I called the surgeon's office to make an appointment with another partner to find out whether my margins were clear or not. Of course, the rude girl answered the phone—just my luck. I explained what I was calling for and explained that I knew my surgeon was out of town, but I just wanted to get the results of the lumpectomy. I knew the nurse or doctor had to give me the results, so all I wanted to do was make an appointment. The front desk girl would not budge. I was so frustrated. I knew I was not going to get the results of my biopsy and knew I could not wait on my surgeon to get back from vacation. Knowing the results were in, but not able to get them, was awful.

Although I do not like pulling the "I'm a dentist" card, it was a necessary time to do it. I called someone very high up in the hospital, who knew me, and knew I was in the medical profession, and they were able to get the results for me. The person who gave me the information was a physician, so it was not like it was just anyone giving me the results.

After hearing the results of the biopsy, I was sad to hear that one of the margins was not clear, which meant I needed another lumpectomy. I reluctantly made an appointment with the breast surgeon. I say reluctantly because I did not like how I was treated by the front desk personnel. I had no doubt that the surgeon was skilled and wonderful, but I just wanted everyone to be nice. I had no patience to deal with the front desk personnel.

At my follow-up appointment with the breast surgeon, I told on myself about how I had to get those results and I apologized for going over their heads. The surgeon and I went over my options—another lumpectomy or a mastectomy. If I did a mastectomy, would I choose a bilateral or unilateral mastectomy? My gut instinct, what was best for me medically, was a mastectomy. The breast surgeon supported my decision and recommended a plastic surgeon in town to consult with me. The plastic surgeon came highly recommended by not only my breast surgeon but my OB-GYN.

When I made an appointment with the plastic surgeon, the ladies working at the front desk were super nice. Robert came with me to the appointment. I wanted to have his objective view on my options. The plastic surgeon came in, and I informed him I wanted a mastectomy with reconstruction. The look on his face when I told him I wanted a mastectomy instead of another lumpectomy was one of disgust, and I think he even rolled his eyes at me. I was shocked, to say the least. He told me in front of Robert that, "Only women who did not care about their breasts would choose the mastectomy," when given the option of doing another lumpectomy. I was shocked. There I was, an intelligent woman, who wanted to do what was best for herself medically long-term, and it was shocking to me that the local plastic surgeon was not on the same page as I was. I had four children who needed their mother to be around. I never wanted to worry about my right breast again, so I felt that a mastectomy was the best decision for me.

As a dentist, I give my patients all of their options, and I go over what I think will give them the best and most long-term results. I already knew I did not want that plastic surgeon to touch me. I did not question his surgical skills at all, but I only wanted people with positive attitudes, who respected my decisions, and who were on board with the treatment I chose. I let the surgeon finish talking, but I wanted to run out (or in my case roll out) as fast as possible. I did not schedule an appointment, and I politely gave a fake smile and thanked the surgeon for his time.

As soon as Robert and I got in the car, he quickly told me that he was not impressed at all with the plastic surgeon and I needed to call the doctor in New Orleans who placed my second set of breast implants, Dr. Michael Moses. Looking back, I should have called Dr. Moses immediately and gone to him first. However, I was trying to stay in Baton Rouge and not fight the traffic back and forth to New Orleans. I knew he was the best choice. His office got me in quickly. As soon as I got off the elevator and was in the doctor's beautiful office, I knew I was in the right place and could kick myself for even wasting my time with another surgeon.

Dr. Moses listened patiently to every detail and recommended a mastectomy. However, I was shocked when Dr. Moses told me he wanted to refer me to another surgeon. He gave me a list of surgeons. He thanked me for my confidence and told me if I met with one of these other surgeons he recommended and I did not like them, then he would do my surgery. But, he was confident that I would like the other surgeons he recommended. He volunteered to personally call and make an appointment for me. After making a few phone calls, he was able to get me in to see Dr. Frank DellaCroce and Dr. Alan Stolier at the Center for Restorative Breast Surgery in New Orleans, just a few days later. I left with the intentions of not liking the surgeon he referred me to and having Dr. Moses do my surgery. In my mind, it was hard to imagine anyone being more amazing than him.

I looked at the website for the Center for Restorative Breast Surgery and St. Charles Surgical Hospital. After one look at their website, I knew I was headed to the right place. I coordinated my appointment with Sutton's appointment with the ENT at Children's Hospital in New Orleans. One amazing and important fact about God—if you are not on the right path, He will put you on the right path, but you have to be aware and look for the signs and trust Him. Easier said than done, but looking back is when we often learn to trust Him, and this helps prepare us for trusting God looking ahead. It takes practice and time. But things happen for a reason.

The second I entered the Center for Restorative Breast Surgery, I was in complete awe. I was at peace. I knew I was in the right place. I had "good" chills. I knew God had a hand in this, and I knew at that moment, before even meeting the doctor, that this facility and this doctor were where I was supposed to be. It was a blessing that the plastic surgeon in Baton Rouge and I were not on the same page, because it led me to the place where I should have been. The center was immaculate. It was clean and very modern. It was peaceful and state-of-the art. The lady who greeted me at the front desk was so friendly. She smiled, stood up to greet me and introduced herself. She was happy and full of joy and positive energy. She was a breath of fresh air. She told me the doctors at the center did her surgery and people from all over the world came to the center. The center was so organized and efficient. Everyone knew what was going on and it ran like a well-oiled wheel.

I met with my new breast surgeon and then with the restorative breast surgeon. I was impressed with how clean the facilities were. I also was impressed when the doctors actually washed their hands in front of me. Both doctors were very detail-oriented, compassionate, extremely intelligent, confident, and humbly proud of the outcomes of their surgeries. They believed in mastectomies only and not lumpectomies, and they told me that they always performed sentinel node biopsies on every patient. The center gathered all records on each patient before every initial appointment so the surgeons could review all of the information prior to coming into the room for the first time. Both doctors took their time examining me. They both explained my options and every detail. They told me the recuperation time was eight weeks or more, and I would have multiple drains in my chest and abdomen, depending on what surgery I decided to have. They also explained the follow-up surgery a year later to revise scars and perform the final "touch-ups." My only decision was whether I wanted a bilateral mastectomy or a unilateral mastectomy with a flap and immediate reconstruction. The left breast would have some minor surgery to make me even. Thank God, I was a candidate for a nipple-sparing/skin-sparing mastectomy due to the location of my cancer. The only thing I needed to decide was if I wanted both breasts removed or one. Either way, I knew I was in the right place and was still in awe of how God guided me there.

I agonized over which surgery to have. One day, I wanted both breasts removed, and the next day I wanted just one removed. I saw before and after photos of the surgeons' work and knew esthetically that I would look great either way. I spent a few weeks going back and forth and had trouble making a decision. I finally chose to only remove my right breast and have immediate reconstruction with the flap, and scar revisions and touch-ups to be done one year later. At the time of the mastectomy, the team of surgeons would change out my left implant to match the right flap and I would have a few "nips and tucks." The best part was that they needed to take tissue and a piece of an artery from my abdomen, so a tummy tuck would be involved. With the mastectomy on only one breast with the flap procedure, it required a four- to five-day stay in the hospital.

I scheduled the surgery for August 2012. A few weeks after scheduling my surgery, I received a call from the center and was informed that they had to move my surgery a week sooner than what was originally scheduled. I was quite frustrated, since my coworkers rearranged my patients and had already blocked my schedule at work. However, I did not have much of a choice since I needed to have the surgery.

With the new surgery date set sooner, the schedule and timeline for everything, from blood work to a CT of my abdomen, required the wonderful ladies who worked the front desk at my office to once again re-arrange patients. I still was adamant that I did not want anyone else to know other than those who already knew. I wanted to protect my children and my mom, and I wanted to keep life as normal for myself as possible. I also wanted to protect my business. So many people in the medical/dental community gossip, and they would have said I was either not working or I was retired, without ever stopping to find out the truth. I knew I had to protect my business and maintain my privacy. Most importantly, I wanted to rely on God to be my strength and not on people. I wanted to trust God and really grow in my walk with Him and not fill my life with what people would tell me.

Don't get me wrong—the support and privacy my inner circle of friends provided was imperative for me. I somehow started thinking of how movie stars must feel about trying to maintain their privacy and how sad it was that so many people gossiped and spread rumors and how miserable that must be that they could not trust anyone around them. I was blessed with a great group of close friends.

Instead of having all the pre-op work done in Baton Rouge, I chose to have everything taken care of at St. Charles Surgical Hospital. The day before my surgery, I was to report there for bloodwork, a chest x-ray, a CT of my abdomen, blood pressure, etc. I had to have a lung function study since I would be in surgery for nine hours or longer, and I did have that in Baton Rouge. But everything else was done at the center in New Orleans the day before my surgery. Robert brought me for my pre-op work up. Then, I had him drop me off at the hotel in downtown New Orleans so he could get back home to our four children and work the next day. I told Robert that I felt better if he worked and ran the office, since this would reduce my worrying about us both missing work. The downfall of owning a small business was that the government does not care if I had cancer and missed work—they still wanted their taxes. There was no box on my income tax forms to check saying I had cancer and needed a little break on my taxes, so, unfortunately, we both could not miss work. I would be less stressed knowing the office was running smoothly and that Robert would be home with the children at night.

My friends (Britta, Monica, and Gwen) decided they would come to New Orleans the evening before my surgery, and we made it a girls' night out, with strict instructions of nothing to eat or drink after midnight. We checked into our hotel, The Saint, in New Orleans, and we had an amazing steak dinner at Dickie Brennan's in the French Quarter. I prepared a letter, prior to my surgery, of instructions for my funeral in case I did not make it through, and I emailed this to Monica. However, I knew deep down that I would be okay and God would not have led me there if I was going to die in surgery. A night at the hotel with my three amazing best friends and a great meal got my mind off of the thought of having my right breast cut out.

The morning of my surgery, my friends and I all arrived at the hospital. I was excited to show them all how amazing and beautiful the facility was. I was not excited about having my breast cut off, but since it had to be done, I was happy I was in an amazing facility surrounded by world-class physicians and nurses.

The nurses told us that since I was in a wheelchair, and since Britta and Monica were both staying with me, they were putting me in a large suite after surgery overlooking St. Charles Avenue. It would give us all more room. We all looked at each other and I said, "Too bad it is not Mardi Gras." We would have the prime spot, being directly on a parade route.

The nurses were all busy prepping me for surgery, and my surgeons came in, along with the anesthesiologist. Before the nurses rolled me out, Britta, Gwen, and Monica all grabbed my hands and prayed for me. They were upbeat and positive, and I was glad they were there. Britta and Gwen left to go to work, and Monica stayed with me. I was thankful for their presence. I was also thankful that Robert honored my wishes and kept the office running and was home at night with the children.

I do not remember the recovery room at all, but I do remember waking up in a huge, beautiful room with large French doors going from where my hospital bed was to a parlor area with large windows and a table, sofa and chairs. The room was so beautiful that I felt like I was either in Heaven or at a luxurious spa. Although I was on an IV with major sedation and narcotics, I remember telling myself that these doctors at this center did this right. I must say the recovery process was faster in a well-decorated, clean, state-of-the-art facility like the one I was in, along with a staff of people who were caring, compassionate and took pride in their jobs. My eyes were only open long enough to admire the facility, and then I slept for what felt like days.

I kept asking Monica about the results of the sentinel node biopsy, but she never answered me. I remember being upset that Monica would not answer me. I remember the nurses coming in a few times to check my re-routed inframammary artery going to my right breast flap with the Doppler to ensure the blood flow was good, but other than that, I had the best sleep ever. I remember my plastic surgeon, Dr. DellaCroce, came in and said in his sweet, compassionate voice, "Well, hello, Sleeping Beauty."

At some point later that morning, the breast surgeon, Dr. Stolier, came in my suite. He asked me how I was feeling and told me I would be pleased with my breasts. He then took my hand and talked to me. He told me it was their standard of care that they performed a sentinel node biopsy on every patient at their facility and that my sentinel node biopsy was positive for cancer. He proceeded to tell me they had to remove eighteen lymph nodes. Two were positive for cancer and I would need chemotherapy for one year. How could this be when my lumpectomy showed DCIS, which was basically a stage 0 cancer? I went from thinking I had a stage 0 cancer to finding out my cancer was a stage 2.

My doctor had tears in his eyes, but they never fell down his face. He was confident that I would be fine, and he sent in the sweet receptionist who I bonded with the first day at my consult to talk with me. Monica cried. I cried. That sweet receptionist was also a social worker or counselor of some sort. And as I mentioned earlier in a previous chapter, she was a breast cancer survivor. She consoled me and gave me a great pep talk, and she told me I was in good hands and had chosen the right facility. She hugged me, held my hand, and was such a positive person.

After about an hour or less of crying and talking with Monica and the receptionist/social worker, I was fine. They cheered me up and had me smiling. Britta arrived later that evening after getting off of work. Both Britta and Monica took care of me for the next four or five days of my hospital stay. Their acts of kindness were selfless—they both had husbands and children, yet they both were there for me every step of the way. True unconditional love. Robert was working full-time at the office during the day, just as I asked, and taking care of four children in the evenings.

I must also add that this amazing facility had a Coca-Cola ICEE machine. I rarely drink soft drinks, but when your best friend goes down the hall and brings you a Coca-Cola ICEE after being told you had cancer in your lymph nodes, and after having a massive sore throat from a long, major surgery, and after crying for a long time, the world just gets a little more wonderful. After my short pity party, I looked back over the past few months and could see God's hand guiding me. At that very moment, I knew in my heart that I was going to beat cancer and I would be fine and that God was not finished with me quite yet.

Over the course of the next four or five days, I remember waking up after a deep sleep in the hospital and hearing Britta talking to Monica and Gwen about how she was upset and angry that I refused to tell my mom and children, and how I refused to make an announcement that I had cancer. I was so sedated and out of it, I could not talk. My surgeons wanted me to rest and stay as still as possible, hence the heavy sedation. At first, my feelings were hurt.

However, one thing I have learned over the years by being friends with them was that they each truly had my best interests at heart, and they each wanted what was best for me and vice versa. I knew Britta's heart was in the right place, and I could understand her point of view. I knew she always wanted what was best for me. I knew that my request to maintain my privacy was out of the box and not what society would think was normal. Just because I understood her point of view did not mean I had to agree with her. But, as her friend, I respected her opinion and understood that she had always been there for me. She feared I was in denial that I had cancer.

I treasure the open communication I have with my close friends.

I quickly realized that most people would feel the way Britta did—meaning that it was not unreasonable to think that I was in denial—but I knew that I was not in denial and knew I needed to protect my children and my privacy. In addition, I wanted to rely on

God emotionally and spiritually—especially if it was my time to die an earthly death. I wanted to be spiritually strong and grow as close to God as possible. I needed and wanted to be the rock that I knew my children, husband, family, friends, and co-workers needed me to be. If it were my time to go, I wanted to die an earthly death as gracefully as possible, with a smile on my face, and I wanted people to see Jesus in me. Therefore, spiritually, I needed to fully rely on God.

I decided after I was out of the hospital, I would sit down with Britta and Monica separately, over dinner, and share my heart to prove I was not in denial. I also wanted to listen to their side and have an open and honest conversation.

A few days after being released from the hospital, an amazing thing happened. I mentioned previously how the center called to move my surgery sooner. Well, guess what? There was a hurricane in South Louisiana the week I originally scheduled to have my surgery, so my surgery would have been canceled due to the hurricane and re-scheduled a few weeks later. So, all that frustration I had because my surgery was moved up was in reality divine intervention for me. God's hand was guiding me, but I could not see it until after the fact.

I still go through periods of not trusting God fully, even when I know He takes care of every little detail and intervenes for my good. Everything I interpreted as bad things were really blessings in disguise—all in God's perfect plan. God knew what I needed before I needed it. God knew who I needed in my life and placed all these people in my life before I even knew I needed them. His ways are perfect—it only requires opening our spiritual eyes.

Chapter Ten

"Do not fear [anything], for I am with you;
Do not be afraid, for I am your God. I will
strengthen you, be assured I will help you;
I will certainly take hold of you with My
righteous right hand [a hand of justice, of
power, of victory, of salvation]."

Isaiah 41:10 AMP

IN THE PROCESS OF HEALING FROM MY MASTEC-
tomy and immediate reconstruction, I had to find a
surgeon to place a Mediport so I could start chemotherapy when I was completely healed from my surgery. My chemotherapy lasted for twelve months. Six
of those months, I had the *bad* chemo, which meant
the chemo caused my hair to fall out. The remaining
six months were *good* chemo, which meant Herceptin-
only chemo and not the chemo that made my hair fall
out. Herceptin is a chemotherapy drug used to treat
HER2 receptor positive cancer.

Since no one was expecting to find cancer in my
lymph nodes, a Mediport could not be placed during my

mastectomy and reconstruction surgery. A Mediport is a port placed under my skin for the IV used during chemotherapy to connect. One would think that if a surgeon is cutting off my right breast and reconstructing it and found positive lymph nodes that it would be all right for him to place the Mediport. However, thanks to all the legal *red tape*, my surgeon was unable to proceed with placing a port, since consent for that must be obtained prior to surgery. Therefore, I needed another surgery to place my port after I healed from my mastectomy with immediate reconstruction.

My oncologist referred me to a general surgeon in Baton Rouge, and I was scheduled to have my Mediport placed in October of 2012. I wanted to wait until after a cruise with my co-workers before I started chemotherapy. Medically, I should not have postponed my chemo for that long. However, the trip was important to me. Had I known my friends and I would be involved in a bus accident on the way to the cruise ship terminal, I would never have gone on the cruise, but unfortunately, life does not work that way.

My privacy was of utmost importance to me, but I had no idea how to do this when I was going to lose my hair within a few weeks of starting chemo. So, I decided to make an appointment with my amazing former hair stylist, John Malta, in New Orleans, to see what ideas he had for me prior to losing my hair. He then scheduled an appointment for me at a wig shop in the French Quarter, Fifi Mahony's. Everyone, from cancer patients to drag queens, purchased their wigs there. The stylist at Fifi Mahony's suggested I purchase two wigs, so I would still have one when I mailed the other one to the wig shop to be washed and styled. Robert went with me as I was fitted for a wig, which I started wearing before I started chemo. My hairstylist colored my hair to match the wig, so that prior to wearing the wig, no one would notice anything had changed.

To be fun and silly when I was out of town where no one knew me, I ordered a red wig—a deep, dark auburn color. I always wanted to color my hair to look like Kate Walsh, but I was never brave enough, so that was my chance.

When my wigs came in, I had an appointment where I learned how to style my wig and how to wear it over my hair before it fell out. If I would have known how easy it was to wear a wig and how good my hair looked, I would have bought a wig a long time ago. My wig was longer than my natural hair, so I had to figure out a way to tell everyone how my hair got an inch or two longer. I did not want to lie, but I decided once I started wearing my wig I would tell my children and my mom that I got extensions.

My wigs came in weeks prior to the placement of my Mediport. Immediately after waking up in the recovery room from having my port placed and being discharged, I had my first chemo treatment. Due to the ridiculous terms of my insurance policy, my Mediport was placed at a different hospital than the one my oncologist's office was in. So, I had to leave one hospital and go directly to another one. Since my surgery was delayed at the hospital where my port was placed, and since I was quite nauseated after my Mediport placement, this caused me to be late for my first chemotherapy treatment. Dr. Castine's office was not going to be able to see me for my first three to four-hour chemo. I was so upset and angry and emotional. I completely understood. However, I had already blocked my schedule and canceled a few patients and was mentally prepared to have chemo that day. I also scheduled to have the following day off.

I remember calling Dr. Castine's nurse, and I am embarrassed to tell you that I was so rude and demanding to him. Keep in mind that my oncologist's nurse was one of the singers at Healing Place Church. Little did I know that he would be one of the four singers I chose to sing at Sutton's service. Anyway, I acted like a donkey to him. I basically threw an adult temper tantrum. As emotionally and as spiritually strong as I am, I am guilty of having adult temper tantrums every now and then. I am human, and life gets overwhelming for all of us, so I acted out—absolutely no excuse for how I treated him, since it was not his fault. I literally begged him to let me come to my first chemo appointment. I am thankful that Dr. Castine and his nurse worked it out to where I could come. I was so grateful to them and to the wonderful nurses in the chemo room.

Looking back, I am shocked they accommodated me due to my un-Christian behavior.

Although I was very sedated from my surgery for placing my Mediport, I remember Monica driving me from the first hospital over to the hospital where Dr. Castine's office was. I remember checking in at the front desk and filling out the sheet with my name and date of birth and checking off the little spot showing I was there for chemotherapy. It felt so weird and unreal that I was marking down that I was at the doctor's office for chemotherapy. I was thirty-nine years old. Cancer was not what a thirty-nine-year-old was supposed to have. I remember wheeling myself back to the chemo room with the help of Monica and Britta. The room was large and open, with a lot of windows. There were comfortable black leather/faux-leather recliners, televisions, an area for snacks, a restroom and a nurses' station. Dr. Castine's office did a fantastic job of preparing me for chemotherapy prior to my first treatment. I met with the nurse practitioner and social worker. They showed me around and I met the nurses in the chemo room and learned the process. My first chemo treatment was over three hours. Each session after that would be three hours every three weeks.

I went into the chemo room, and it was full of older patients. I was the youngest patient in the chemo room. My biggest concern for my first chemo session was finding a spot that I wanted to sit in for three hours. It was kind of like going to church and scoping out the best possible place to sit, with the understanding that the spot I chose would be *my spot* for the next year. *My spot* or an available recliner near *my spot* was available almost every time I went, and luckily, I only had to sit on the opposite side of the room one time within my year of chemo. I chose *my spot* near the corner of the room, based on the simple fact that it was less crowded in that area. Also, I wanted to sit in front of the windows facing the entrance of the chemo room so I could see everyone walking in—it was the best spot for people watching!

I remember every patient in the room that first day turned to look at me. Their eyes had such compassion for me. It sounds crazy, but there was something about the chemo room that allowed me to feel the compassion of others. I felt it deep within my soul. I, in turn, felt great compassion for every one of those people in the chemo room with me. Most of the patients who received chemo that day were sixty and older. People from all different backgrounds, all different ages and from all walks of life. We all sat in one room, each of us in the most comfortable recliner ever, hooked up to IV bags, which hung from each of our poles. Each pole connected the tubes to the ports in our chests, and all of us experienced chemotherapy together. Without one word uttered, I felt so much love in the room, yet I felt so much sadness and pain as well.

From the evening that I arrived home after my Mediport placement/first chemo treatment, through the next three days, I had the best sleep I ever had. I stayed in bed almost the entire weekend sleeping. I remember my older three children coming in the master bedroom, wanting to see me, and I remember Robert having to keep them out so I could sleep. I remember hearing Mason, who was seven years old at the time, cry because she wanted to see me. I remember the older three children wanting to know why I was in bed so long. This was very out of character for me. I questioned myself and wondered if I was making the right decision by not telling my children I had cancer. After going over everything, I felt in my heart it was best for my children, best for me, and best for my business to continue to maintain my privacy.

By the Monday after my first chemo, just four days later, I was back at work. I felt great. I guess all those steroids made me feel amazing. Thank God for scrubs, is all I can say, for they hid my Mediport scar and hid the bulge in my skin where it was obvious I had a port. And thank God that the first weekend after chemo was pretty much the only time I was in bed all weekend. And thank God that the massive doses of steroids that I was given decreased my neck pain from the injury I had sustained in the bus accident. I was happy I felt well enough to go trick-or-treating with all four children and Robert in my friend Melanie's neighborhood, less than a week after my first chemo.

Chapter Eleven

"I have told you these things, so that in Me
you may have [perfect] peace. In the world
you will have tribulation and distress and
suffering, but be courageous [be confident, be undaunted, be filled with joy]; I
have overcome the world. [My conquest is
accomplished, My victory abiding.]"

John 16:33 AMP

I REMEMBER ALL TOO WELL THE DAY THAT I HAD TO start wearing my wig. It was almost three full weeks after I started chemo. Melanie and I were on our way to a high school state swim meet to watch Bennett and her daughter swim. We were walking to the parking lot. It was cold and windy outside. Melanie was walking behind me when the wind blew hard. Reluctantly, she had to tell me that a handful of my hair fell out from the back of my head and landed on her sweatshirt. She could see my scalp. I could tell by the sound and tone in her sweet voice that she hated to tell me that, but she knew I wanted to maintain my privacy.

The weekend we arrived home, Robert kindly and politely told me that he hated to tell me, but it was time for me to start wearing my wig full-time. He suggested I call my hair stylist in Baton Rouge, Lindsey, and have her shave my head. I knew it was time to do this when handfuls of my hair were falling out when I washed my hair. My scalp looked like a dog that had mange.

Lindsey was gracious enough to see me after hours, when no one else was in the salon. My heart hurt and ached when I saw her using the electric clippers and shaving away all my hair where I was almost bald. Losing my hair was harder on me emotionally than having a mastectomy with reconstruction. Even though I had a fabulous wig, I felt so ugly bald. I was not a pretty bald woman at all. You know how some men and women look beautiful with a bald head because they have a perfectly shaped head? Well, I did not look good bald. Suddenly, I went from a very confident woman to a very self-conscious woman within seconds of losing my hair. Nothing beneath my surface changed—only my surface changed. However, I felt like a different person without my hair. I felt weak emotionally for being so upset about something so trivial and so shallow. It wasn't until Lindsey put my wig on and styled my hair that I felt normal.

That night, after all four of my children went to bed, I locked my bedroom door, undressed in my bathroom, and I had one more step in my nightly routine now—to take off my wig and take off the stocking that went under my wig so that the wig did not scratch my head. I cried as I soaked in the bathtub. I cried more over losing my hair than I did when my doctor told me I had cancer in my lymph nodes. Robert asked, hesitantly, and in a very respectful way if he could shave my head with a razor, something Lindsey could not do in her salon. He did not want what little hair that was left to fall out and get in my eyes accidentally, so I let him put shaving cream on my head and use a razor. I cried even more.

When I got married and took the "in sickness and health" part of my vows, I never would have envisioned or imagined that I would ever have cancer and would be sitting in my bathtub, sobbing as my husband shaved my head. After my little pity party, I knew I had to gain control of my emotions and be strong for my four children. I prayed to God to give me the strength and courage I could only get from Him. I suddenly had a "let's do this" attitude. I got out of the tub and dried myself off— tears and all—and put my happy face on. I climbed out of the emotional rut that I was in, changed my attitude to a positive one, and decided with God's help, I had to press on with life and to make life as normal as possible for my children, myself and for my co-workers.

I decided, for the first time ever, that I would start locking the door to the master bedroom in case one of the older three children would come in during the middle of the night or in the morning when Robert and

I were sleeping late, so that they would not be startled and scared if they saw me without hair. Sutton had a crib in our room and was so little that he was the only one of my children who saw me without hair. Remembering to lock my bedroom door at night was difficult, but I quickly got in the habit of it.

I must admit that as soon as my bald head hit my pillow for the first time, it felt like Heaven on my head. I did not realize how amazing my head could feel without hair. My doctor suggested wearing a soft cotton hat at night to keep the heat in, but I didn't feel the need. Only on cold nights would I sleep with a hat on my head. It did not take long for me to adjust to wearing a wig. When I realized how much later I could sleep in the mornings without having to wash my hair and blow dry it, I was thrilled. I would rather not have had cancer, of course, but there was at least something positive. At work, my sweet co-workers made sure that my wig was always on straight each time I took off my mask or safety goggles. They all had their own little way of communicating with me that my wig needed to be adjusted if it was in front of a patient. Fortunately, a few of my co-workers worked with me long enough to come up to me and straighten my wig for me if patients were not around. My biggest concern was that Sutton would grab my hair and accidentally pull my wig off. He was the only person besides Robert and a few others I allowed to see me without my wig. Sutton would laugh hysterically when he saw me take my wig off.

I quickly became adjusted to wearing a wig. Within just a few days of wearing a wig to work and being out and about around town, I began learning what living beneath my surface was all about. I became very aware of how people treated each other and how people responded to others. Wearing a wig and being an undercover cancer patient made me more aware of how I treated others and how I responded to others. Would the rude cashier at the store be nicer to me if she knew I had cancer? Would the waiter at the restaurant be a little more patient with me if he knew I had cancer? Would the person I was on the phone with use a nicer tone if he knew I had cancer? However, I learned I needed to turn these questions around and ask myself the same questions. If I really knew what was going on beneath the cashier's surface, would I be nicer to her? If I really knew what was going on in the waiter's life, would I be more understanding and patient with him? If I knew the details of the lives of the people I encountered daily, would I respond differently to them? Would my attitude and tone be nicer if I knew what was going on beneath their surface? My point is that we all are going through things that cannot be seen on our surface. Some, like me, are just really good at hiding and masking what is going on beneath the surface.

As quickly as I adjusted to wearing a wig, I adjusted just as quickly to the routine of going to chemo. Thankfully, I missed very little work from chemo. Each time I went to chemo, I prayed no one asked me my name or what I did for a living. I did not want anyone to "blow my cover." I tried to keep to myself instead of talking to the person in the recliner next to me. When I did talk, I tried to give as little information about myself as I could. There were times I would sit and listen to the older patients. Some of them made me laugh hysterically.

One day, there were about four elderly patients, all over the age of seventy, talking about how nauseated they were and how they were going to buy some marijuana for their nausea. As soon as the nurses were not around to listen, these elderly patients all said they had never done drugs before, but were so sick and could not stop throwing up. They looked at me and asked if I wanted to come with them. I was shocked that four elderly people would ask me to go with them to buy marijuana. I politely declined and told them I had never done drugs before and was certainly not going to start. I was never even offered drugs in college, and there I was in the chemo room, having people old enough to be my grandparents ask me if I wanted to go buy illegal drugs. I still laugh about how they asked me, like a, "Pssst, do you want to come with us to buy marijuana to help with nausea?" Yes, I was still naïve, and I had no idea of how to even go about doing so and whom to ask, and here were the seventy-plus-year-olds knowing where to go.

I quickly learned how much fun it was to listen to some of their stories. I listened as one elderly man told another elderly man about some of his promiscuous behaviors "back in the day," and listened to conversations of how some of their families abandoned them and did not come and visit, as well as heart-warming stories of how much they loved their families. Some days, it was like I was listening to a radio version of a soap opera. I honestly had some great laughs and heard some great stories in the chemo room. I could have easily written a book, entitled *Tales from the Chemo Room*, that would have made people laugh and cry.

I brought books to read in the chemo room—all self-help books. I then started bringing my laptop and writing about my cancer journey. After my fifth miscarriage, I had felt God leading me to write a book about the pain and isolation I felt after each miscarriage, but I literally laughed at the idea and questioned God. I was a scientist and dentist and not a writer. I pushed the still, quiet voice aside. For years, I pushed that calling aside. However, the more self-help books and devotionals I read and the more my relationship with God grew, the more I felt the Holy Spirit lead me to write a book about my cancer journey and what I learned spiritually. Again, I felt inadequate writing a book, but having three hours every three weeks to sit in a recliner hooked up to the chemo pole and do nothing forced me to listen to God. And so, I began the journey of writing this book.

I was very relieved that the first six months of bad chemo were much better than I expected, and much easier than I could ever have imagined. I was blessed not to be tired and not be sick like most people were. I was more nauseated with each pregnancy than I was with chemo. However, my oncologist's office did a great job with making sure they gave me anti-nausea medicine prophylactically. They were also great about giving IV fluids if any of their chemo patients felt like we needed fluids. The massive doses of steroids made me feel great and full of energy. The steroids made me hungry, and I ate an ungodly amount of food and felt hungry all of the time. In addition to the steroids making me hungry, one of the chemo drugs caused the lining of my stomach to slough off, which caused my brain to think I was hungry. So, between the steroids and chemo, I always felt hungry no matter how much I ate. Other than the first weekend after chemo, I felt hungry for a year even though I ate plenty of food.

Unfortunately, I had to have several injections of Neulasta, a medicine that increases white blood cell production, which causes deep, horrible bone pain for a few days. The fact I had to sign a piece of paper stating if my insurance company did not cover this injection, I would owe $4,000 per shot, was way more painful than the pain I felt in my bones from the injection! I am thankful my insurance covered the injections. Besides prayers, fluids, and steroids, I attributed the fact that I felt better during chemo than I expected to my positive attitude as well as the positive attitudes of my inner circle of friends and my amazing co-workers. I also appreciated the fact that Robert kept the office and house running smoothly as if nothing was wrong.

After six months of bad chemo, my oncologist referred me to a radiation oncologist to make sure I did not need radiation. I was grateful to learn that no radiation was needed, which was fantastic news since every single person in the chemo room told me how horrible it was. I then had six months of easy chemo. On October 10, 2013, I completed my last chemo treatment.

In the chemo room, I met so many amazing nurses, team members, and patients. There was this unspoken bond between chemo patients. I am not sure if other people going through chemo will agree with me. They may even think what I am saying is crazy, but I think there is an unspoken bond. It is hard to describe, but it is like even though we were all from different walks of life, we were all walking through hell together, yet we all had hope and we all knew what each other was going through and could relate to each other without one word being spoken. There was an unspoken sense of compassion for one another and a sense of "we are all in the same boat" type of bond. I can also say I have never been in the presence of this many patient people. It seemed to me that I was the only impatient person in the oncologist's office, and learning patience was definitely an area I needed to improve on. Every single person I came in contact with at my oncologist's office, whether it is a patient or someone working in his office, was so patient. I had never seen anything like it.

Being in the chemo room was God's way of forcing me to relax and to have time to self-reflect, think, step away from my life for just a short time, and spend time with God and myself. Of course, I never want to have cancer or chemo ever again, and I do not wish cancer on anyone, but for me, it took me having cancer to appreciate life. How sad for me to say that, but it is the truth. Some of the people I met in the chemo room were so inspiring, and I am sad that I will never know the outcome of their treatment. All I can do for them is pray that God will heal them and pray that they find peace with this awful disease.

Finishing chemo was somewhat overwhelming. It was as if I looked back and asked myself, "Did this just really happen to me?"

After chemo was over, my oncologist then ordered a PET scan (a full body scan) to make sure I was cancer-free before scheduling my second phase of breast reconstruction. I was sad to learn my insurance company refused to pay for my PET scan. Apparently, the analyst at the insurance company did not feel it was medically necessary before they paid for my Mediport to be removed and my second stage of reconstruction performed.

On October 24, 2013, my very skilled and talented plastic surgeon performed the second phase of reconstruction. The second stage of reconstruction involved removing my Mediport, a few "nips" and "tucks," scar revisions, and making sure both of my breasts were even. There is no doubt in my mind that part of the reason my cancer journey was so much easier than most was because of Dr. Frank DellaCroce and Dr. Alan Stolier and because of the environment at St. Charles Surgical Hospital, as well as the nurses and team at the hospital. Words cannot describe how awesome that place was. Having my surgery at this world-class facility was effortless and definitely helped alleviate my stress. The suite on St. Charles Avenue was not available to put me in. However, the ICEE machine made up for it. I spent one night in the hospital, and Monica brought me home the next day. I was on the road to recovery and officially being cancer-free (thank You, sweet baby Jesus)!

I must say being an undercover cancer patient was extremely unique and eye-opening. And quoting Britta, I cannot believe I "pulled it off." My decision to not share my cancer diagnosis with others had been a very controversial subject amongst my closest friends, and it might even be controversial in this book. However, I made the decision to do what was best for me and what was best for my children and my business. I would not have had the peace I needed to survive Sutton's tragic death if I would have let the world in and not relied on God for my strength. My journey was between God and me, and it was something I had to deal with on a spiritual level.

My hope and prayer is that after people in my life who did not know about my journey find out, then they will see how God carried me through, how God guided me and how God gave me peace, which ultimately prepared me for Sutton's death. God always knows what we need before we even know we need it.

Being in the chemo room for three hours every three weeks taught me a lot. As odd as it may sound, I grew up in the chemo room, meaning I matured. I found myself. I discovered what really mattered in life. Being in that room changed me for the better and put me on a different path. It brought me closer to God.

Looking back, I thank God I had cancer, because God used that situation to spiritually prepare me for losing Sutton. I feel that life is a test, and there are many bad things that happen in everyone's life. In my opinion, every one of these trials is meant for us to learn something. I feel that what we all learn from these life lessons are meant to prepare us for Heaven, to prepare us to help others, to make us better individuals, and to make us stronger to handle the next trial in life.

As crazy as it sounds, having cancer forced me to slow down for a few hours every three weeks, which was slow enough for God to teach me so many things. I learned about myself. I learned that I was much stronger and more determined than I thought. I self-reflected over my life—examining the details on both good and bad choices I made—and could see how I should have handled things differently or how I could have improved in many areas or how I could have treated people better. I learned that everyone has "stuff" going on in their lives that I do not see, and these things going on in our lives affect how we all respond to each other. At first glance, it was so easy for me to sit around and "point the finger" at others and judge and criticize and find ways for them to change. However, knowing that we all have things going on beneath the surface made it easier to see what I must change about myself instead.

I could not change others. I had to change myself. I had to stop and analyze my actions and my decisions and analyze my attitudes and find ways to improve myself. I learned to look at others with more empathy and compassion than I already had. I learned that what I see on the surface of others is not necessarily what reality is, so I try to get to a person's center and look past what I see on the exterior and look beneath their surface. I do my best to change my attitude and actions in a more postive way no matter how people treat me or respond to me. I do not always succeed, and I make mistakes daily. However, I am at least aware that I need to improve.

Having cancer forced me to acknowledge the reality of me dying soon and forced me to grow spiritually to a place I would never have been able to achieve without that time in the chemo room. My spiritual growth during this time was only possible because of a sermon Pastor Dino Rizzo preached a year or two prior to my cancer diagnosis. Because of his sermon, I made a life-altering decision to join a Bible study group. Pastor Dino challenged the church one Sunday to "get out of the row and into a circle." He challenged each person in the church to choose a Bible study group or *Connect Group* at church, and just commit to going for three meetings. He promised it would "change your life." I decided I would go only if I looked through the list of options for people leading the *Connect Group* and found someone I knew. The only name on the list I recognized was Dr. Cheri LeBlanc, so I decided to sign up Robert and me. My plan was to only go for three meetings and fulfill the challenge. Obviously, God had a different plan.

Pastors Dino Rizzo and Mike Haman prepared a DVD for the small group Bible studies for each of the three meetings. I watched the video series with my *Connect Group*. In one of the videos, Pastor Mike said, "Life is made up of tests." To sum up the DVD, he said, "The good news is that we will never fail the test," but "the bad news is that if we do not pass the test on the first try, we have to repeat the test." He really explained this well, and I heard his message loud and clear. Listening to his sermon really was a turning point for me as far as how I viewed life. I started viewing trials as life lessons to prepare me for Heaven.

I pray that I am not faced with cancer ever again, and I pray that I learned whatever life lessons God wanted me to learn in the chemo room. Did I "pass" my test that can never be failed, or will I have to "repeat" my test? Only time will tell.

During my entire cancer journey, I constantly searched for what I was supposed to learn from this journey. I felt writing the details of my journey was important and that my story was meant to help someone. Deep down in my soul, I felt God telling me to write a book about my journey. I have heard and felt this for a very long time. However, I kept ignoring that little voice inside me because it sounded so ridiculous to me. I am a dentist with absolutely no background in journalism and no background in writing anything that is worth publishing. Yet, that little voice inside me telling me to write a book kept getting stronger and stronger, and it became so strong that I could not ignore it.

I would write for a few weeks and then stop, and then write and stop. After Sutton went to Heaven, the tug on my heart to write this book became stronger and stronger. Halfway through writing this book, I decided I was not a writer and it was ridiculous that God would ask me to write a book. But that changed when I went to a Christian concert in Baton Rouge where Big Daddy Weave, We Are Messengers, and Zach Williams were playing. Before the concert, a man in one of the bands (Darren from We Are Messengers) came up to me and told me, "God has a message for you tonight if you are willing to listen." At the close of the concert, a man stood up in front of everyone and said "If you were the woman in the wheelchair that Darren talked to before the concert, he wants to talk to you privately if you are willing to meet with him. He has a message for you." As silly as it was, I questioned whether he was talking about me or not. I looked around, and as usual, I was the only female in the building who had a wheelchair. I moved from my seat to meet him.

Darren took his hands and gently but firmly put them on my face, looked me in the eyes, and confidently asked me, "What is God asking you to do? Tell me what He has asked you to do. He wants you to finish what He has asked you to do," he passionately said.

I sobbed, for I knew exactly what God was telling me through Darren. I had never met this man before, and here God was using Darren to deliver a clear and powerful message to me. As I cried, I told Darren, "God has called me to write a book, and I need to finish it."

Darren asked me what the book was about, and I told him. We talked for about twenty minutes, and we both cried. Then, Darren and another lady prayed with me that I would have the perseverance to finish this book.

I now know I can persevere through anything if I have faith in Him. With God, anything is possible. I have always said this and always preached this to my children, but for the first time in my life, I truly believe it. I always said the words and thought I believed the words, but I finally understand the words, "With God, anything is possible," because I have lived it. To truly understand something or understand an experience, one must live it. And, I have most definitely lived both the hills and the valleys of life.

I would not have made it through my cancer journey if it would not have been for my amazing inner circle of friends and sister, my wonderful co-workers, Bible study group from church, and without Robert supporting my decision to maintain my privacy and keep everything as normal as possible. I really feel that the few family members and friends who I chose to tell about my cancer have "carried my cross" during this. I think that they have been way more upset and have taken the fact that I had cancer much harder than I did. Galatians 6:2 (NIV) states "Carry each other's burdens, and in this way you will fulfill the law of Christ." Therefore, I give all the credit for my peace and excellent results, both surgically and spiritually, to God and to my inner circle praying for me and being there for me.

I beat cancer and am very thankful to God for carrying me through this. I look back over my life, and I get very overwhelmed thinking about the valleys I have lived through. I am thankful that my outlook on life changed for the better in the chemo room. I am thankful that I changed. I am thankful I learned to rely on God spiritually and to trust Him.

I look back and see that the only reason I made it through this was due to God's mercy, grace and guidance. I also had a fantastic oncologist and great surgeons and wonderful family, friends and co-workers who supported me and prayed for me and honored my wishes to protect my children and my privacy. My mom and children now know I had cancer. I told them shortly before this book went to print.

I am humbled that God healed me and gave me peace, but in an odd way, I also have some type of "survivor's guilt," if that makes any sense. I keep asking myself why God spared me. Why did God choose me to be healed and not the other people I have known or met or read about dying from cancer? Why did God take Sutton and not me? Although I do not know the answer and may never know the answer, I must trust that God has a reason. I do believe in my heart one day, when I get to Heaven, God will unfold the big picture, and I will know the reasons. For now, I must trust the fact that He is not finished with me yet.

Chapter Twelve

"Brothers and sisters, I do not consider that I have made it my own yet; but one thing I do: forgetting what lies behind and reaching forward to what lies ahead, I press on toward the goal to win the [heavenly] prize of the upward call of God in Christ Jesus."   Philippians 3:13-14 AMP

THE MESSAGE OF THIS BOOK IS NOT TO CONDEMN—the message I hope to share is that, while it may be hard to make a positive change in the world, all that hard work pays off when it helps save lives through more training, more funding, and raising salaries for emergency responders. These actions help motivate people to learn more and prevent devastating accidents from happening. Cutting through the red tape of politics, and finding the right people to sit down with and have an honest discussion on how to change, instead of hiding from hard conversations, takes courage, but on the other side of courage is change. My prayer is that by sharing my story, I can help others begin to look at their lives, self-reflect, and see that even amidst the pain, suffering, illnesses, anger, frustration, and tragedies, God does have a plan for everyone's lives.

I believe every life is important and has purpose and meaning. I also think that counseling is imperative. In the hands of a great counselor and/or a pastor/spiritual leader, talking with someone and learning coping strategies helps tremendously. I challenge each person to grow spiritually knowing that God is always with you. When faced with life's storms, I try my best to learn as much as possible through the trials, no matter how weary and hopeless I feel.

I know what it feels like to have a huge void in my heart! I live with a void in my heart every day. I know what pain and suffering and heartache feel like. I know how much the sadness hurts. I know how deep the grief feels. I know how it feels to be so isolated and alone, even though I have very supportive and amazing people surrounding me. I know what it feels like to cry in the bathtub by myself, to cry myself to sleep, and have so many tears pouring out of my eyes that I cannot see and can barely breathe.

I am here to share that no amount of money, no title in front of or behind my name, no house no matter how large and no matter how fancy, no nice car, no piece of jewelry no matter how beautiful and expensive, no expensive purse and no person on earth can fill that void and fill that deep pain in my life like God the Father/God the Son/ God the Holy Spirit can. I am not alone. God is with me and sees me and is with me every step of the way, and He sees every single person and is with us on this journey. My circumstances are different. My journeys are different. However, I learned that beneath the surface, we all have more similarities than differences.

I believe no one can genuinely touch another person's heart and get to their center and look beneath their surface and no one can love another person unconditionally until each of us can self-reflect and can look deep into our own heart—our entire heart—the ugly part and the good part—and get to our own center and finally learn to love ourselves the way God loves us. And I am here to say that no person in this earthly world can love you more than you love yourself. Once I truly understood God's love for me and understood how much God loves me, then I learned to love myself. And because I love myself, I can love my neighbor as myself, as Mark 12:31 states.

I can look back and see how God has prepared me every step of the way. Within the blink of an eye, my world was shattered, as soon as I heard the ER physician tell me that Sutton did not make it. It felt like my heart was ripped out of my body. I experienced (and continue to experience) the most unbearable pain deep down in my soul—an ache, a longing for Sutton, a pain that runs so deep that it takes my breath away, a pain that I wish no one ever had to experience. I feel stuck between Heaven and Earth. On one hand, my heart cannot wait to see Jesus and cannot wait to see Sutton and my dad again, along with the rest of my loved ones. However, on the other hand, my heart wants to be here with Bennett, Palmer and Mason and watch them grow up. Each day, my heart feels torn between this longing for Heaven and this longing to be with my other three children here on earth. However, like Pastor Levi Lusko has said in one of his podcast sermons, "We are not made for this world," so it is natural and normal for each of us to want to be with Jesus in Heaven and return to the source of life.

Sutton was so full of pure, innocent love, and reminded me daily of God's unconditional love for us. I am so grateful to God for choosing me to be Sutton's mom. Although my pain over losing Sutton is very deep, I would not trade the joy and love Sutton brought to my heart and into my life during the four short years he was here for anything. Life here is short, and I took it for granted by always thinking that there would be a tomorrow when, in reality, my life changed in a second.

There will come a time in everyone's life when they will feel shattered and like their hearts have been ripped into pieces. I encourage each person to live each day as if it were the last, and to never leave things unsaid. I encourage each person reading this to not worry about what other people think. I can say from experience, when I lived my life based on what other people said about me and thought about me, it felt like I lived in a self-inflicted prison. I encourage each person to listen to what God is saying, for He has a plan for all of our lives. I feel that it is imperative that none of us holds in what we feel God wants us to say or do, for fear of being rejected or dismissed. Leaving things unsaid only leads to regret. If the opportunity is missed, none of us will ever get that time again. I no longer save the fine china for a special day, for tomorrow may never come. I no longer let my circumstances rob me of my joy. I try to live life to the fullest. It is time for each of us to wake up, open our spiritual eyes and see that this world is not our home, and live for today!

Although I have had so many storms in my life, I can look back and see how God has used each of those storms to help prepare me for not only losing my son, but to give me the strength and courage to write this book and help others see that there is beauty and peace in the aftermath of life's storms. There is beauty in the ashes.

I grieve with hope, knowing deep down in my heart that I will see Sutton again when I get to Heaven. I grieve knowing Sutton's life had a purpose and that Sutton fulfilled his destiny, and I grieve knowing that Sutton's life positively impacted so many lives.

Although I do not like this journey God has put my family and me on, I do have faith in Him and trust that everything that happens is for a higher, more divine purpose. One day, I will understand God's plan. Through this journey, I have learned that life is not only about loving, but life is also about growing and learning and understanding life lessons and growing in our faith, no matter how tragic and painful our circumstances are. I know that each of us has a destiny to fulfill, and each of us has a purpose in life, and everyone's life has meaning. In this crazy, dark world we live in, there is chaos all around us. The chaos and negativity of the media, the newspapers, social media, politicians arguing, senseless killings, racial tensions, hate crimes, and the list goes on and on.

Thanks to Pastors Dino Rizzo and Mike Haman, I now grasp the concept they preach about how "hurt people, hurt people." We all hurt inside. However, all of the chaos going on in the world and in our lives is just a distraction by the enemy to keep each one of us from fulfilling our destinies and to prevent us from fulfilling our purpose in life. We all forget that everyone makes mistakes. We forget that we all are interconnected, and we forget that we must accept one another and respect one another and value life. We need to accept that each one of us is unique and marvel in our uniqueness and work together and help each other. Once these concepts are understood, healing begins. There is no better feeling than a healed heart that was once broken!

I feel this huge responsibility in my heart to send a message of love and peace and to challenge people, including myself, to find their inner lights and let their lights shine and send a positive message to this broken world. It often takes unfortunate events or even tragedies in life to learn this, so I learned to embrace these events and seek God and ask Him to teach me what I am supposed to learn from every circumstance, so that I may learn and grown and hopefully be a light to others.

My prayer for everyone reading this book is that my life and Sutton's life and his beautiful smile be a reminder to spread God's unconditional love and joy.

Go out and let your light shine! Be the change you are looking for, and fulfill your destiny!

"But the righteous one, though he die early, shall
be at rest.
For the age that is honorable comes not with the
passing of time,
nor can it be measured in terms of years.
Rather, understanding passes for gray hair,
and an unsullied life is the attainment of old age.
The one who pleased God was loved,
living among sinners, was transported—
Snatched away, lest wickedness pervert his mind
or deceit beguile his soul;
For the witchery of paltry things obscures
what is right
and the whirl of desire transforms the innocent mind.
Having become perfect in a short while,
he reached the fullness of a long career;
for his soul was pleasing to the Lord,
therefore he sped him out of the midst of wickedness.
But the people saw and did not understand,
nor did they take that consideration into account."

Wisdom 4:7-14 NABRE

There once was a child
with the brightest of smiles
And a mop of curly, golden hair.
He had love for everyone
And touched hearts everywhere.
He was our gift,
a lovely present from God.
So we must be thankful for him,
But we miss the sunshine of his laughter
And life seems lonely and dim.
There is a child named
Sutton Reed Bruns
Now in his Heavenly Father's care.
He will talk and smile through eternity,
Making everything brighter up there.

Poem written by Kim Burleson

Resources

ALTHOUGH MY FAITH IN GOD IS STRONG, I MUST constantly work on growing spiritually and being mindful of making the time to work on strengthening my relationship with God. I must make time daily to renew my mind, heart, and spirit and to protect myself from the darkness in the world.

Listed below are categories of books, devotionals, music, etc. that have helped me on my spiritual journey. God used these means to help heal my broken heart. I did not list every book or sermon I listened to—the list would be too long. These are just a few of my favorites. Everyone is so different—what works for me may not work for someone else. I felt led to at least give a list of what worked for me to give some sort of starting point for anyone who may be interested on where and how to start allowing God to heal your soul.

These books, devotionals, etc. are not meant to take the place of counseling or take the place of seeking the advice of a medical professional. I highly suggest talking to a pastor, priest, licensed counselor, or seeing a physician if needed.

Books

Joyce Meyer
The Confident Mom
Knowing God Intimately
Battlefield of the Mind
Living Beyond Your Feelings

Dr. Gary Chapman
Anger: Taming a Powerful Emotion
The 5 Love Languages

Matthew Kelly
The Seven Levels of Intimacy

Dr. Mary Neal
To Heaven and Back

Lysa TerKeurst
Uninvited: Living Loved When You Feel Less Than, Left Out and Lonely

Devotionals

Joyce Meyer
Power Thoughts Devotional
Love Out Loud
Hearing from God Each Morning

Priscilla Shirer
  The Armor of God

John Bevere with Addison Bevere
  The Holy Spirit: An Introduction

Sarah Young
  Jesus Calling

The YouVersion Bible App

The Bible app has hundreds of devotionals to choose from. I search under a topic and find one that appeals to me. The app allows me to sample a plan before starting it. The best part is that there is no charge for this Bible app! I have a few friends I trust and who I can be completely honest and open with, and we do these plans together. I may have two or three plans going on at one time with two or three different people, and we will text each other our comments or answers each day. If we get behind, we catch up when we can. These Bible studies are easy and quick and can easily be incorporated into your daily living. I learn something new each day!

Music

I try and start my morning with positive, uplifting music as well as a short devotional. I listen to music in the morning when getting dressed in the morning for work, when I am driving, throughout the day as I work, and when getting dressed in the evening before I go to sleep. Positive, uplifting music is a huge part of my life and helps me so much. It refreshes my soul. Thank you to the following artists for your music! Music carried me through some dark days and nights. There were some nights after Sutton went to Heaven that I would cry for hours in the middle of the night and listen to some of these songs over and over and over again until the words were stuck in my heart and in my head. I focused on the words to help work through my pain and cried out to God to help me.

Please note: with so many Christian artists singing each other's songs, it is often difficult to know which artist sings what song. I did my best to match them correctly, but the last thing I want is to have something be inaccurate!

Bethel
"Seas of Crimson"

Big Daddy Weave
"My Story"
"Overwhelmed"
"Redeemed"

Chris Tomlin
"Amazing Grace (My Chains are Gone)"

"How Great Is Our God"
"Lay Me Down"
"Our God"

Colton Dixon
"Through It All"

Crowder
"Come As You Are"
"Forgiven"

Francesca Battistelli
"Holy Spirit"

Hillsong Worship
"Age to Age" (featuring Brooke Fraser)
"Oceans"

Jason Gray
"Remind Me Who I Am"

Jesus Culture
"Love Has a Name"

Kari Jobe
"Forever"
"Heal Our Land"
"I Am Not Alone"

King & Country
"Shoulders"

Lauren Daigle
"First"
"How Can It Be"
"Trust In You"
"Loyal"
"My Revival"
"Salt & Light"

Mandisa
"Overcomer"
"Unfinished"

Matt Redman
"Blessed Be Your Name"
"10,000 Reasons"

Mercy Me
"Flawless"
"I Can Only Imagine"
"Word Of God Speak"

Michael W. Smith
"A New Hallelujah"
"Healing Rain"
"Sky Spills Over"

Plumb

    "God Help Me"

    "Lord I'm Ready Now"

    "Need You Now (How Many Times"

Ryan Stevenson

    "Eye of the Storm"

Steven Curtis Chapman

    "Glorious Unfolding"

    "Love Take Me Over"

Third Day

    "Soul On Fire"

    "Praise the Invisible"

    "Spirit"

We are Messengers

    "Dancing in the Dark"

    "Everything Comes Alive"

    "Magnify'

    "Point to You"

Zach Williams

    "Chain Breaker"

Inspirational Speakers

Attending church regularly (or as regularly as possible) at my church home is imperative to my life. When I am out of town, I try to watch my church online or visit a church in the city I am in. Filling my spirit with a positive message was vital to God healing my heart. The chaotic world drains me, and I refuse to let the enemy rob my joy. I watch sermons on podcasts and YouTube, and on the app for Healing Place Church. I listen to sermons by Beth Moore, Christine Caine, Dino Rizzo, Joel Osteen, John Gray, Joyce Meyer, Levi Lusko, and Mike Haman.

The four-part "Through the Eyes of a Lion" podcast by Levi Lusko helped me tremendously.

Acknowledgments

UPON COMPLETION OF THIS BOOK, I HAD A VERY overwhelming moment. I could look back on my entire life and see all the AMAZING people God placed in my life to help guide me, teach me, and mold me into the person I am today. God also blessed me with some wonderful and intelligent physicians and health care providers. I was truly in awe of how many people that have gone above and beyond to help my family and me. It would be impossible for me to list every name. However, I wanted to say thank you from the bottom of my heart to the wonderful people listed below. For anyone I inadvertently left out, thank you as well.

To my parents, Barney (deceased 2007) and Katharine Bennett: thank you for raising Tammy and me in a loving, peaceful, Christian home. Thank you for the sacrifices you made for both of us. Thank you for paying for me to attend a Christian high school.

To Bennett, Palmer, and Mason: God has a purpose for each of your lives. I pray you seek His will for your lives and keep God in the center of your relationships. You bring such joy to my life. I love each one of you!

To Robert: thank you for being a great dad, for working so hard and keeping the office going in my absence, for always cooking, and for maintaining my privacy during my cancer journey. Thank you for keeping life as normal as possible for me. You are one of the smartest people I know and are a fantastic dentist. God has blessed you with the ability to restore people's smiles, and that is life-changing for so many. We have lived an incredible life and have had so much fun, but we have also been through a tremendous amount of heartache. When we married, I never thought in a million years we would ever be in this position. Thank you for all you do. I am sorry for the heartache I have caused you.

To my sister, Tammy Bennett and my niece, Misty May Beaudine: I love you. Thank you for your love, support, and prayers. Tammy, thank you for designing the book cover! You are a very talented artist and graphic designer! I am so proud of you! For more information on the graphic designer of this cover, please visit <u>tammybennett.myportfolio.com</u>.

To Pastors Dino and DeLynn Rizzo and Mike and Rachel Haman and everyone at Healing Place Church: I am grateful for your leadership, sermons, prayers, and support. You each have a beautiful heart. Pastor Dino, thank you for your "Get out of the row and into a circle" challenge! You were right—it changed my life! I also am grateful for the amazing service you all gave Sutton. Thank you to the HPC band for your incredible music.

To Brothers Jim Efferson, Sam LoBello, and Marvin Collins, and all my Sunday School teachers at Park Forest Baptist Church: thank you for your spiritual guidance and showing me the love of God at such a young age.

To my *Connect Group* at Healing Place Church— Dr. Cheri LeBlanc, Joe LeBlanc, Teresa and Shawn Rougon, Julie and Stu Broussard, Marylyn and John Cadwallader, Ann and David Ziegler, and Jacci and Lonnie Bickford: thank you for teaching me your spiritual wisdom and knowledge. Thank you for showing me the love of Jesus. This group changed my life in a positive and powerful way.

To Vicki McGuire and Susan Ragan, the best high school English teachers a girl could ask for: this book would not have been possible without your excellent teaching skills (as well as the talented editors who proofread this book). Forgive me for any grammatical errors!

To my teachers at Park Forest Elementary, Parkview Baptist School, and at the other schools and universities I attended: thank you for educating me and doing it so well.

To the teachers, faculty, staff, parents, and students at Episcopal High School: thank you for stepping up and helping Bennett, Palmer, and Mason during this tragic time in their lives. I love the diversity of the school and how Episcopal does such a great job of teaching the children to put their differences aside and reach out and love and support people and show that we are alike in so many ways. I was in awe of how everyone rallied around my family and came together in unity to help. I am forever grateful!

To Monica Lyon Davis: I am so grateful you are in my life. You loved and accepted me when I did not even love myself. I appreciate your spiritual guidance and your beautiful, compassionate heart. I have learned so much from you. Thank you for being such a positive influence and an amazing, loyal friend. You know I love you.

To Britta Rabalais Wilson: I am so grateful for you. You taught me to love myself and helped shape me into being a confident woman and taught me how to not worry about what anyone else thought. I am forever grateful. You are a true definition of a Sigma Sigma Sigma sister and friend. It has been a great journey watching the friendship between Monica, you, and me grow into an unbreakable bond. You know how I feel about you!

To Kim Robinson Guidry: I appreciate your friendship, love, and support! Your help at my house during the weeks after Sutton went to Heaven is very much appreciated. The day we spent together crying, talking, taking naps, and reminiscing about our college days is a memory I will treasure forever!

To Gwen Corbett: thank you for being my friend. I appreciate your wisdom and honesty on both a personal and professional level. You are an amazing friend, dentist, mother, and person. You help make my world so much better!

To Darren Mulligan from We Are Messengers: thank you for delivering that message God laid on your heart the night of your concert in Baton Rouge! Your obedience in sharing what God laid on your heart motivated me to complete this book.

To my amazing, loyal, and fun co-workers at Bruns Family Dental Center: Deborah Conerly, David Miley, Brittany Robb Mayeux, Britta Rabalais Wilson, Stephanie Neilsen, Jennifer Mollere, Monica Lyon Davis, Anne-Marie Zito Soileau, Bethany Creel Sunde, Erica Wheat, Adrienne Champagne, and Cheryl Campesi Ranlett. Thank you for your excellent level of patient care, for maintaining my privacy, and for making work fun. Your love, support, prayers, and laughter make coming to work a true joy.

To Darelle Deslatte Bergeron, T.J. Bergeron, Jenna Nicol, Skyler Simoneaux, Courtney Karam, Suzanne Miller Rogers, and Brittany Knox: thank you for loving my children like your own and taking amazing care of them.

To Dianne Evans, Wendy Evans Chapman, Kasey Evans Quibodeaux, and Dustin Quibodeaux: you know my family and I love and adore each of you. Thank you for all you do for us. Dustin, special thanks to you and Ourso Funeral Home for taking such great care of Sutton.

To Melanie Turnley: I treasure our friendship. You are an incredible friend, and I enjoy every moment we are together. I appreciate your love and support.

To Dianne Morris Rathcke: thank you for being there for me and listening to me. I love and appreciate you so much. I value our friendship.

To Sandy and Craig Merrill: thank you for being part of my family and for loving my children like your own. Thank you for your prayers, loyalty, and love.

To my wonderful friends: Dr. Ann Zedlitz, Dr. Trent Massengale, Dr. Lisa Gautreau, David Gautreau, Sheri and Bobby Mckey, Tim and Teresa Normand, Jennifer and David Jarreau, Luci and Wayne Stabiler, Ashley and Billy Potter, Tina and Keith Russell, Gayle and Joe Martin, and everyone else that helped the night Sutton went to Heaven as well as the days, weeks, months, and years later. Thank you for everything you did for my family and me.

To Kelli and Dennis Pennington: thank your friendship, for all the Thanksgiving dinners we had at your house, for your help at the memorial service, for having the logo designed for The Sutton Bruns Foundation, and for the paperwork for the foundation. You both are amazing people.

To Brenda and Keith Catha, and the rest of the gang in the dinner club: thank you for your prayers and for the fun gatherings at restaurants and your boat dock parties.

To Molly Quirk: thank you for reminding me to get my mammogram. God placed you in my life that day. You helped give me more time on earth with my children. Thank you! I am forever grateful for you!

To Craig Davidson, Leah Scott, and Tracy Rome: thank you for your hard work and for always listening to me! I am grateful for each one of you! Thank you for all of your help and encouragement!

To Lyle LeBlanc: Thanks to you being my best friend growing up, I have great childhood memories. You were the most perfect best friend I could have asked for! I know we do not see each other due to our busy schedules, but I am so proud of you and am thankful for you.

To Shane Miller: I am grateful for your friendship! You are like the brother I never had, and I think we are twins separated at birth (ha-ha). I enjoy our conversations! You are an amazing friend.

To the people that have gone through the loss of a child who have supported me throughout this journey: thank you. Special thanks to Paula Roussel Crowe (Jordan's mom), Marla and Jim Cobb (The Burke Cobb Foundation), Dara Bertucci (Cheering for Breanna Foundation), Kim and Trey Bowman (The Bella Bowman Foundation), and Jane Barney (Blake's mom). I could not have gone through this heartbreaking journey without your honesty and guidance.

To my Sigma Sigma Sigma sisters at Southeastern Louisiana University: thank you for taking a young, nerdy, and unconfident girl (me) and giving her the love and support she needed to blossom into the confident woman I am today. Your acceptance of me was life-changing. I love each and every one of you. Special thanks to Britta Rabalais Wilson, Kim Robinson Guidry, Shari Arnold, and Jennifer Flynn Jouandot.

To Lisa Scalia Landesman, D.D.S., Christy Dryden, D.D.S., and Robin Chatman Shannon, D.D.S.: thank you for all you did for me in school.

To Claudia Cavallino, D.D.S. and the Louisiana State University School of Dentistry Class of 2002: thank you for arranging all the dentists to fill in for Robert and me during the two weeks we were off work. Our practice could not have survived without your help. To the dentists who filled in for us that I never thanked, I appreciate your taking the time off from your busy practices to help. Claudia, you are an amazing leader, dentist, and person.

To Dr. Sharon Lee, Pam Passantino, Nita Marcum Lindsly, Mona Wheat, and Brandi LeBlanc at Louisiana Women's Healthcare: thank you for taking great care of me during my pregnancies with Bennett, Palmer, Mason, and Sutton. Your level of care and compassion is incredible. I am so appreciative of you, Dr. Lee, for ordering my mammograms at age 35! You helped save my life on earth for a little longer. I love each of you!

Dr. Bobby Webster and Nancy Webster, and Dr. Duane Superneau: I thank you and your team along with God for giving me Sutton. I am eternally grateful.

To my chiropractor, Dr. Robert Smith at Baton Rouge Chiropractic and Nutrition: thank you for your countless hours of working on me and helping me get answers.

To Dr. Thos Evans, Dr. Donald Corenman, Lori Fugate, Elena Hernandez, and the rest of the team at The Steadman Clinic and Vail Valley Medical Center: thank you for your phenomenal orthopedic state-of-the-art medical facilities. There is no other place like it. Thank you for your practice philosophy of keeping people active and for helping me!

To Dr. Frank DellaCroce, Dr. Alan Stolier, and the rest of the team at the Center for Restorative Breast Surgery and St. Charles Surgical Hospital: thank you for helping to save my life and for your impeccable surgical skills. Thank you for restoring me! I am proud and honored to be your patient, and I am grateful for your world-class facilities and for your dedication to women going through breast cancer. Thank you to Dr. Michael Moses for giving me all of my options!

To my oncologist, Dr. Michael Castine, the wonderful nurses in the chemo room, and every team member in your office: thank you for making my cancer journey easy and for helping to save my life. Dr. Castine, you are an incredible oncologist and person and have a great office.

To Eddie Austin, P.T., Christine Perkins, O.T., Michelle Chellew, P.T., Christian Coulon, P.T., Lana, Rob, Brooklyn, and the entire Physical Medicine department at the Baton Rouge General Bluebonnet: thank you for help and excellent patient-centered care you provide.

To Dr. Robert Burris and Dr. Steven Sotile at Woman's Hospital: thank you for your excellent care.

To Dr. Michael Leahy: thank you for taking great care of me.

To Ian Lusins, Chris Wall, and Melissa Monroe McGehee at Trinity Holistic Health and Training: thank you for your help teaching me good exercise habits and good eating habits. I love and appreciate each of you!

To Kenneth Clark, Erika Bennett, Jennifer Kasper, Kimberly Ludwig, Lorelei Martinsnek, and everyone at Xulon Press who worked on this book from editing to printing to marketing: thank you for your help and guidance and for your patience with me in learning the process of writing a book. I appreciate each of you.

To John Malta at John Malta Salon, Lindsey Rabalais Delhommer at Studio des Amis, and everyone at FiFi Mahoney's: thank you for the fabulous hair and wigs.

To the therapists and team members with the Early Steps program, Neurotherapy Specialists, and EMERGE: thank you for your countless hours working with Sutton and for loving him. Sutton loved and adored each of you.

To Sutton's teachers, Ginger Deroche and Melanie Sandahl, and Principal Mary Sue Slack and everyone at Southdowns Elementary: thank you for everything you did for Sutton. Your school was a true blessing to Sutton.

To Kym Heine, M.S. and everyone at Prentke Romich Company: thank you for giving Sutton a voice! Your AAC device is truly amazing. I am so thankful for your company and your dedication to helping give Sutton a way to communicate.

To Karen Khonsari: thank you for all you did for us after Sutton passed away. I appreciate your friendship.

To Chief Deron Pat Wilson, Chris Lowe, Maria Navia, and Mark Griffin and the entire Coweta County Fire Department and community: thank you for your help and your donations to the flood relief efforts.

To Joyce Meyer, Christine Caine, John Gray, Beth Moore, Levi Lusko, and Joel Osteen: although I have never met you, I wanted to thank you for your sermons, words of inspiration, books, as well as thank you for your ministries. Thank you for doing what God has called you to do. God used your inspiring words to comfort me when I was at my lowest point in life. Thank you!

To K-LOVE Radio: thank you for always playing positive and encouraging music.

To my friends who let me come write at your house so I could have a quiet place to work: thank you. You hold a special place in my heart.

For more information about this book
and about the author, please visit:
www.KristaBennettBruns.com
or email the author at
krista@kristabennettbruns.com

A portion of the proceeds from this book will go to:
The Sutton Bruns Foundation

TheSuttonBrunsFoundation.Org